MEDITERRANEAN COOKBOOK

Publications International, Ltd.

Pictured on the back cover *(clockwise from top left)*: Pomegranate Chicken Wings *(page 72)*, Chicken Cassoulet *(page 77)* and Flatbread with Herbed Ricotta, Peaches and Arugula *(page 155)*.

Photograph on front cover copyright © Shutterstock.com.

ISBN: 978-1-68022-995-0

Manufactured in China.

8 7 6 5 4 3 2 1

Microwave Cooking: Microwave ovens vary in wattage. Use the cooking times as guidelines and check for doneness before adding more time.

CONTENTS

SMALL PLATES

BRUSCHETTA

MAKES 1 CUP (8 SERVINGS)

4 plum tomatoes, seeded and diced

½ cup packed fresh basil leaves, finely chopped

5 tablespoons olive oil, divided

2 cloves garlic, minced

2 teaspoons finely chopped oil-packed sun-dried tomatoes

¼ teaspoon salt

⅛ teaspoon black pepper

16 slices Italian bread

2 tablespoons grated Parmesan cheese

1. Combine diced tomatoes, basil, 3 tablespoons oil, garlic, sun-dried tomatoes, salt and pepper in large bowl; mix well. Let stand at room temperature 1 hour to blend flavors.

2. Preheat oven to 375°F. Place bread on baking sheet. Brush remaining 2 tablespoons oil over one side of each bread slice; sprinkle with cheese. Bake 6 to 8 minutes or until toasted.

3. Top each bread slice with 1 tablespoon tomato mixture.

MANCHEGO CHEESE CROQUETTES

¼ cup (½ stick) butter

1 tablespoon minced shallot or onion

½ cup all-purpose flour

¾ cup milk

½ cup grated manchego cheese or Parmesan cheese, divided

¼ teaspoon salt

¼ teaspoon smoked paprika or paprika

⅛ teaspoon ground nutmeg

1 egg

½ cup plain dry bread crumbs

Vegetable oil

1. Melt butter in medium skillet over medium heat. Add shallot; cook and stir 2 minutes. Stir in flour; cook and stir 2 minutes. Gradually whisk in milk; cook until mixture comes to a boil. Remove from heat. Stir in ¼ cup cheese, salt, paprika and nutmeg. Transfer mixture to small bowl; cover and refrigerate several hours or up to 24 hours.

2. Shape teaspoonfuls of dough into 1-inch balls with lightly floured hands.

3. Beat egg in shallow bowl. Combine bread crumbs and remaining ¼ cup cheese in second shallow bowl. Dip each ball into egg, then roll in bread crumb mixture.

4. Heat ¼ cup oil in medium skillet over medium-high heat. Cook croquettes in batches until brown on all sides, replenishing oil as needed. Drain on paper towels. Serve warm.

TIP: Cooked croquettes may be kept warm in a 200°F oven up to 30 minutes before serving.

SERRANO-WRAPPED SHRIMP WITH LIME SAUCE

MAKES 6 TO 8 SERVINGS

¼ cup orange or citrus marmalade

Grated peel and juice of 1 lime

2 tablespoons honey

24 large raw shrimp, peeled and deveined (with tails on)

2 tablespoons fresh lime juice

1 teaspoon ground cumin

½ teaspoon smoked paprika or paprika

8 slices Serrano ham or prosciutto

1 tablespoon olive oil

1. For sauce, combine marmalade, peel and juice of 1 lime and honey in small microwavable bowl. Microwave 1 minute on HIGH; stir well. Set aside.

2. Place shrimp in medium bowl. Add 2 tablespoons lime juice, cumin and paprika; toss to coat.

3. Cut each slice of ham lengthwise into 3 strips. Wrap one piece of ham around each shrimp; thread onto wooden skewer. (Soak skewers 20 minutes in warm water before using to prevent burning.)

4. Heat oil in large nonstick skillet over medium heat. Cook shrimp in batches 2 minutes per side or until ham is golden and shrimp are pink and opaque. Remove from skewers; serve immediately with sauce.

ANTIPASTO WITH MARINATED MUSHROOMS

MAKES 6 TO 8 SERVINGS

Marinated Mushrooms (recipe follows)

4 **teaspoons red wine vinegar**

½ **teaspoon dried basil**

½ **teaspoon dried oregano**

Generous dash black pepper

¼ **cup extra virgin olive oil**

4 **ounces mozzarella cheese, cut into ½-inch cubes**

4 **ounces prosciutto or cooked ham, thinly sliced**

4 **ounces provolone cheese, cut into 2-inch sticks**

1 **jar (10 ounces) pepperoncini peppers, drained**

8 **ounces hard salami, thinly sliced**

2 **jars (6 ounces each) marinated artichoke hearts, drained**

6 **ounces black olives**

1. Prepare Marinated Mushrooms; set aside. Combine vinegar, basil, oregano and black pepper in small bowl. Add oil; whisk until well blended. Add mozzarella cubes; stir to coat. Cover and marinate in refrigerator at least 2 hours.

2. Drain mozzarella cubes, reserving marinade. Wrap 1 prosciutto slice around each provolone stick; roll up remaining slices separately.

3. Arrange mozzarella cubes, prosciutto-wrapped provolone, prosciutto rolls, drained mushrooms, pepperoncini, salami, artichoke hearts and olives on large platter. Drizzle reserved marinade over pepperoncini, artichoke hearts and olives.

MARINATED MUSHROOMS

3 tablespoons fresh lemon juice

2 tablespoons chopped fresh parsley

1 clove garlic, crushed

½ teaspoon salt

¼ teaspoon dried tarragon

⅛ teaspoon black pepper

½ cup extra virgin olive oil

8 ounces small or medium fresh mushrooms, stemmed

Combine lemon juice, parsley, garlic, salt, tarragon and pepper in medium bowl. Whisk in oil until well blended. Add mushrooms; stir to coat. Marinate, covered, in refrigerator 4 hours or overnight, stirring occasionally.

FALAFEL WITH GARLIC TAHINI SAUCE

MAKES 8 SERVINGS

1 cup dried chickpeas, sorted and rinsed

Garlic Tahini Sauce (recipe follows)

1 small onion, chopped

½ cup chopped fresh parsley

2 cloves garlic

1 tablespoon fresh lemon juice

2 teaspoons ground cumin

1 teaspoon ground coriander

½ teaspoon salt

½ teaspoon ground red pepper

Vegetable oil

Pita bread, lettuce, tomatoes, chopped cucumbers (optional)

1. Place chickpeas in large bowl; cover with water by 3 inches. Soak 8 hours or overnight. Prepare Garlic Tahini Sauce; refrigerate until ready to serve.

2. Drain chickpeas; place in food processor. Add onion, parsley, garlic, lemon juice, cumin, coriander, salt and red pepper. Pulse until mixture is smooth, scraping side of bowl frequently. If mixture is too dry, add 1 to 2 tablespoons water.

3. Shape mixture into 1½-inch balls with dampened hands. Place on baking sheet lined with waxed paper.

4. Pour oil into deep heavy saucepan to depth of 2 inches. Heat over medium-high heat to 350°F. Fry falafel in batches 3 to 5 minutes or until golden brown. Remove with slotted spoon and drain on paper towels.

5. Serve with pita bread, lettuce, tomatoes, cucumbers and Garlic Tahini Sauce.

GARLIC TAHINI SAUCE
MAKES ABOUT 1 CUP

½ **cup plain yogurt**

¼ **cup tahini**

3 **tablespoons water**

2 **tablespoons fresh lemon juice**

1 **clove garlic, minced**

½ **teaspoon ground cumin**

Salt and black pepper to taste

Whisk all ingredients in small bowl until well blended. Cover and refrigerate 1 hour.

GOAT CHEESE–STUFFED FIGS

7 **fresh firm ripe figs**

7 **slices prosciutto**

1 **package (4 ounces) goat cheese**
   Ground black pepper

1. Preheat broiler. Line baking sheet or broiler pan with foil. Cut figs in half vertically. Cut prosciutto slices in half lengthwise to create 14 pieces (about 4 inches long and 1 inch wide).

2. Spread 1 teaspoon goat cheese onto cut side of each fig half. Wrap prosciutto slice around fig and goat cheese. Sprinkle with pepper.

3. Broil about 4 minutes or until cheese softens and figs are heated through.

SAVORY PITA CHIPS

MAKES 4 SERVINGS

2 whole wheat or white pita breads
  Olive oil
3 tablespoons grated Parmesan cheese
1 teaspoon dried basil
¼ teaspoon garlic powder

1. Preheat oven to 350°F. Line baking sheet with foil.

2. Carefully cut each pita round in half horizontally; split into two rounds. Cut each round into six wedges.

3. Place wedges, inside layer down, on prepared baking sheet. Brush lightly with oil. Turn over; brush again.

4. Combine Parmesan, basil and garlic powder in small bowl; sprinkle evenly over pita wedges.

5. Bake 12 to 14 minutes or until golden brown. Cool completely.

CINNAMON CRISPS: Substitute melted butter for olive oil and 1 tablespoon sugar mixed with ¼ teaspoon ground cinnamon for Parmesan cheese, basil and garlic powder.

SPANISH TORTILLA

1 teaspoon olive oil

1 cup thinly sliced peeled potato

1 small zucchini, thinly sliced

¼ cup chopped onion

1 clove garlic, minced

1 cup shredded cooked chicken

8 eggs

½ teaspoon salt

½ teaspoon black pepper

¼ teaspoon red pepper flakes

Fresh tomato salsa (optional)

1. Heat oil in 10-inch nonstick skillet over medium-high heat. Add potato, zucchini, onion and garlic; cook and stir about 5 minutes or until potato is tender, turning frequently. Stir in chicken; cook 1 minute.

2. Meanwhile, whisk eggs, salt, black pepper and red pepper flakes in large bowl. Carefully pour egg mixture into skillet. Reduce heat to low. Cover and cook 12 to 15 minutes or until egg mixture is set in center.

3. Loosen edges of tortilla and slide onto large serving platter. Let stand 5 minutes before cutting into wedges or 1-inch cubes. Serve warm or at room temperature. Serve with salsa, if desired.

FISH BITES WITH ROMESCO SAUCE

1 slice crusty Italian bread

1 plum tomato, quartered

3 tablespoons whole blanched almonds

2 cloves garlic, peeled

2 tablespoons chopped pimientos, drained

1 tablespoon red wine vinegar

¼ teaspoon paprika

¼ teaspoon plus ⅛ teaspoon salt, divided

1 egg white

2 tablespoons all-purpose flour

½ teaspoon ground red pepper

⅓ cup ground almonds

8 ounces tilapia fillets

1. Preheat oven to 350°F. Lightly grease two baking sheets or line with parchment paper.

2. For sauce, place bread, tomato, whole almonds and garlic on one baking sheet. Bake 12 to 15 minutes or until almonds are lightly browned. Transfer ingredients to food processor; pulse just until ingredients are coarsely chopped. Add pimientos, vinegar, paprika and ⅛ teaspoon salt. Process until almost smooth. Place sauce in small bowl; set aside.

3. Lightly beat egg white in small bowl. Combine flour, ground red pepper and remaining ¼ teaspoon salt in shallow bowl. Place ground almonds in second shallow bowl.

4. Cut tilapia fillets into four 1½-inch pieces. Coat fish in flour mixture, shaking off excess. Dip into egg white; roll in almonds until evenly coated.

5. Arrange fish on second baking sheet. Bake 18 to 20 minutes or until fish is golden brown and begins to flake when tested with fork. Serve immediately with sauce.

TIP: Slivered almonds can be substituted for the whole almonds. In step 2, bake them on a separate baking pan for 8 minutes or until lightly browned, stirring once.

LAVASH CHIPS WITH ARTICHOKE PESTO

MAKES 6 SERVINGS (ABOUT 1½ CUPS PESTO)

3 **pieces lavash bread, each about 7×9 inches**

¼ **cup plus 2 tablespoons olive oil, divided**

¾ **teaspoon kosher salt, divided**

1 **can (14 ounces) artichoke hearts, rinsed and drained**

½ **cup chopped walnuts, toasted***

¼ **cup packed fresh basil leaves**

1 **clove garlic, minced**

2 **tablespoons fresh lemon juice**

¼ **cup grated Parmesan cheese**

To toast walnuts, spread on ungreased baking sheet. Bake in preheated 350°F oven 6 to 8 minutes or until golden brown, stirring frequently.

1. Preheat oven to 350°F. Line two baking sheets with parchment paper.

2. Brush both sides of each piece lavash with 2 tablespoons oil. Sprinkle with ¼ teaspoon salt. Bake 10 minutes or until lavash is crisp and browned, turning and rotating baking sheets between upper and lower racks after 5 minutes. Cool completely on wire racks.

3. Place artichoke hearts, walnuts, basil, garlic, lemon juice and remaining ½ teaspoon salt in food processor; pulse about 12 times until coarsely chopped. With motor running, add remaining ¼ cup oil in thin steady stream until smooth. Add cheese; pulse until blended.

4. Break lavash into chips. Serve with pesto.

SOUPS

FRENCH LENTIL SOUP

MAKES 4 TO 6 SERVINGS

- 3 tablespoons olive oil
- 1 medium onion, chopped
- 1 carrot, chopped
- 1 stalk celery, chopped
- 1 clove garlic, minced
- 8 ounces dried lentils, rinsed and sorted
- 3 cups vegetable broth
- 1 can (about 14 ounces) stewed tomatoes
- 1 teaspoon balsamic vinegar
  Salt and black pepper
- ½ cup grated Parmesan cheese (optional)

1. Heat oil in large skillet over medium heat. Add onion, carrot, celery and garlic; cook about 9 minutes or until vegetables are tender but not browned, stirring occasionally.

2. Stir in lentils, broth and tomatoes; bring to a boil over high heat. Reduce heat to low; cover and simmer 30 minutes or lentils are until tender.

3. Stir in vinegar and season with salt and pepper. Sprinkle with Parmesan, if desired.

GREEK LEMON AND RICE SOUP

MAKES 6 TO 8 SERVINGS

2 tablespoons butter

⅓ cup minced green onions

6 cups vegetable or chicken broth

⅔ cup uncooked long grain rice

4 eggs

Juice of 1 lemon

⅛ teaspoon white pepper (optional)

1. Melt butter in medium saucepan over medium heat. Add green onions; cook and stir about 3 minutes or until tender.

2. Stir in broth and rice; bring to a boil over medium-high heat. Reduce heat to low; cover and simmer 20 to 25 minutes or until rice is tender.

3. Beat eggs in medium bowl. Stir in lemon juice and ½ cup broth mixture until blended. Gradually pour egg mixture into broth mixture in saucepan, stirring constantly. Cook and stir over low heat 2 to 3 minutes or until soup thickens enough to lightly coat spoon. *Do not boil.* Stir in pepper, if desired.

FRESH TOMATO PASTA SOUP

MAKES 8 SERVINGS

1 tablespoon olive oil

½ cup chopped onion

1 clove garlic, minced

3 pounds fresh tomatoes (about 9 medium), coarsely chopped

3 cups vegetable or chicken broth

1 tablespoon minced fresh basil

1 tablespoon minced fresh marjoram

1 tablespoon minced fresh oregano

1 teaspoon whole fennel seeds

½ teaspoon black pepper

¾ cup uncooked rosamarina, orzo or other small pasta

½ cup (2 ounces) shredded mozzarella cheese

1. Heat oil in large saucepan over medium heat. Add onion and garlic; cook and stir until onion is tender.

2. Add tomatoes, broth, basil, marjoram, oregano, fennel seeds and pepper; bring to a boil. Reduce heat to low; cover and simmer 25 minutes. Remove from heat; cool slightly.

3. Purée tomato mixture in batches in food processor or blender. Return to saucepan; bring to a boil. Add pasta; cook 7 to 9 minutes or until tender. Sprinkle with mozzarella cheese.

ITALIAN PASTA SOUP WITH FENNEL

MAKES 6 SERVINGS

1 tablespoon olive oil

1 small fennel bulb, trimmed and chopped into ¼-inch pieces (1½ cups)

4 cloves garlic, minced

3 cups vegetable broth

1 cup uncooked small shell pasta

1 medium zucchini or yellow summer squash, cut into ½-inch chunks

1 can (about 14 ounces) Italian-seasoned diced tomatoes

¼ cup grated Romano or Parmesan cheese

¼ cup chopped fresh basil

   Black pepper

1. Heat oil in large saucepan over medium heat. Add fennel; cook and stir 5 minutes. Add garlic; cook and stir 30 seconds. Add broth and pasta; bring to a boil over high heat. Reduce heat; simmer 5 minutes. Stir in zucchini; simmer 5 to 7 minutes or until pasta and vegetables are tender.

2. Stir in tomatoes; heat through. Ladle into shallow bowls; top with cheese, basil and black pepper.

GHORMEH SABZI (PERSIAN GREEN STEW)

MAKES 6 SERVINGS

PREP TIME: 35 MINUTES
COOK TIME: 8½ HOURS (LOW) OR
4½ HOURS (HIGH)

- 1½ **pounds boneless leg of lamb, cut into 1-inch cubes**
- 1 **teaspoon ground turmeric**
- ¾ **teaspoon salt, divided**
- ½ **teaspoon curry powder**
- ½ **teaspoon ground black pepper, divided**
- 2 **tablespoons olive oil, divided**
- 2 **medium onions, chopped**
- 1 **bag (5 ounces) fresh baby spinach, chopped**
- 2 **cups chopped fresh Italian parsley**
- 1 **cup chopped fresh cilantro**
- 6 **green onions, green part only, chopped**
- 1½ **cups beef broth**
- 1 **can (about 15 ounces) cannellini beans, drained and rinsed**
- 2 **tablespoons fresh lime juice**
- 3 **cups hot cooked basmati rice**

SLOW COOKER DIRECTIONS

1. Coat inside of slow cooker with nonstick cooking spray.

2. Combine lamb, turmeric, ½ teaspoon salt, curry powder and ¼ teaspoon pepper in large bowl. Heat 1 tablespoon oil in large skillet over medium-high heat. Add half of lamb; cook and stir 4 minutes or until browned. Transfer to slow cooker. Repeat with remaining lamb. Add onions and remaining 1 tablespoon oil to skillet; cook 6 to 7 minutes or until onions are starting to brown. Stir in spinach, parsley, cilantro and green onions; cook and stir 2 minutes or until wilted. Add to lamb in slow cooker; pour broth over all.

3. Cover; cook on LOW 8 hours or on HIGH 4 hours. Add beans. Cover; cook on HIGH 30 minutes. Turn off heat. Stir in lime juice, remaining ¼ teaspoon salt and ¼ teaspoon pepper. Serve over rice.

GREEK-STYLE CHICKEN STEW

MAKES 6 SERVINGS

3 pounds skinless chicken breasts

All-purpose flour

2 tablespoons olive oil, divided

2 cups cubed peeled eggplant

2 cups sliced mushrooms

¾ cup coarsely chopped onion (about 1 medium)

2 cloves garlic, minced

1 teaspoon dried oregano

½ teaspoon dried basil

½ teaspoon dried thyme

2 cups chicken broth

¼ cup dry sherry or additional chicken broth

¼ teaspoon salt

¼ teaspoon black pepper

1 can (14 ounces) artichoke hearts, drained

3 cups hot cooked wide egg noodles

1. Coat chicken very lightly with flour. Heat 1 tablespoon oil in Dutch oven or large nonstick skillet over medium heat. Add chicken; cook 10 to 15 minutes or until browned on all sides. Transfer chicken to plate; drain fat from Dutch oven.

2. Heat remaining 1 tablespoon oil in same Dutch oven over medium heat. Add eggplant, mushrooms, onion, garlic, oregano, basil and thyme; cook and stir 5 minutes.

3. Return chicken to Dutch oven. Stir in broth, sherry, salt and pepper; bring to a boil. Reduce heat to low; cover and simmer 1 hour or until chicken is cooked through. Add artichoke hearts during last 20 minutes of cooking. Serve over noodles.

MEDITERRANEAN CHILI

PREP TIME: 20 MINUTES
COOK TIME: 7 TO 8 HOURS (LOW) OR
3½ TO 4 HOURS (HIGH)

- 2 cans (about 28 ounces each) chickpeas, rinsed and drained
- 1 can (28 ounces) diced tomatoes
- 1 can (about 14 ounces) vegetable broth
- 2 onions, chopped
- 10 kalamata olives, chopped
- 4 cloves garlic, chopped
- 2 teaspoons ground cumin
- ¼ teaspoon ground red pepper
- ½ cup chopped fresh mint
- 1 teaspoon dried oregano
- ½ teaspoon grated lemon peel
- 1 cup crumbled feta cheese

SLOW COOKER DIRECTIONS

1. Combine chickpeas, tomatoes, broth, onions, olives, garlic, cumin and ground red pepper in slow cooker; stir to blend. Cover; cook on LOW 7 to 8 hours or on HIGH 3½ to 4 hours.

2. Stir in chopped mint, oregano and lemon peel; top each serving with feta.

PASTA FAGIOLI SOUP

MAKES 5 TO 6 SERVINGS

PREP TIME: 12 MINUTES
COOK TIME: 4 TO 5 HOURS

- 2 cans (about 14 ounces each) vegetable broth
- 1 can (about 15 ounces) Great Northern beans, rinsed and drained
- 1 can (about 14 ounces) diced tomatoes
- 2 zucchini, quartered lengthwise and sliced
- 1 tablespoon olive oil
- 1½ teaspoons minced garlic
- ½ teaspoon dried basil
- ½ teaspoon dried oregano
- ½ cup uncooked tubetti, ditalini or small shell pasta
- ½ cup garlic seasoned croutons
- ½ cup grated Asiago or Romano cheese
- 3 tablespoons chopped fresh basil or Italian parsley (optional)

SLOW COOKER DIRECTIONS

1. Combine broth, beans, tomatoes, zucchini, oil, garlic, dried basil and oregano in slow cooker; mix well. Cover; cook on LOW 3 to 4 hours.

2. Stir in pasta. Cover; cook on LOW 1 hour or until pasta is tender.

3. Serve soup with croutons and cheese. Garnish with fresh basil.

TIP: Only small pasta varieties like tubetti, ditalini or small shell-shaped pasta should be used in this recipe. The low heat of a slow cooker won't allow larger pasta shapes to cook completely.

MIDDLE EASTERN LENTIL SOUP

2 tablespoons olive oil

1 small onion, chopped

1 medium red bell pepper, chopped

1 teaspoon whole fennel seeds

½ teaspoon ground cumin

¼ teaspoon ground red pepper

4 cups water

1 cup dried lentils, rinsed and sorted

½ teaspoon salt

1 tablespoon fresh lemon juice

½ cup plain yogurt

2 tablespoons chopped fresh parsley

1. Heat oil in large saucepan over medium-high heat until hot. Add onion and bell pepper; cook and stir 5 minutes or until tender. Add fennel seeds, cumin and ground red pepper; cook and stir 1 minute.

2. Add water, lentils and salt. Bring to a boil. Reduce heat to low. Cover and simmer 25 to 30 minutes or until lentils are tender. Stir in lemon juice.

3. Top each serving with yogurt; sprinkle with parsley.

TIP: Serve with homemade pita chips (page 16) or lavash chips (page 22).

STEW PROVENÇAL

MAKES 8 SERVINGS

2 cans (about 14 ounces each) beef broth, divided

⅓ cup all-purpose flour

1 to 2 pork tenderloins (about 2 pounds), trimmed and diced

4 unpeeled red potatoes, cut into cubes

2 cups frozen cut green beans, thawed

1 onion, chopped

2 cloves garlic, minced

1 teaspoon salt

1 teaspoon dried thyme

½ teaspoon black pepper

SLOW COOKER DIRECTIONS

1. Whisk ¾ cup broth and flour in small bowl. Cover and refrigerate.

2. Add remaining broth, pork, potatoes, green beans, onion, garlic, salt, thyme and pepper to slow cooker; mix well.

3. Cover; cook on LOW 8 to 10 hours or on HIGH 4 to 5 hours. Stir flour mixture into slow cooker. Cook, uncovered, 30 minutes or until thickened.

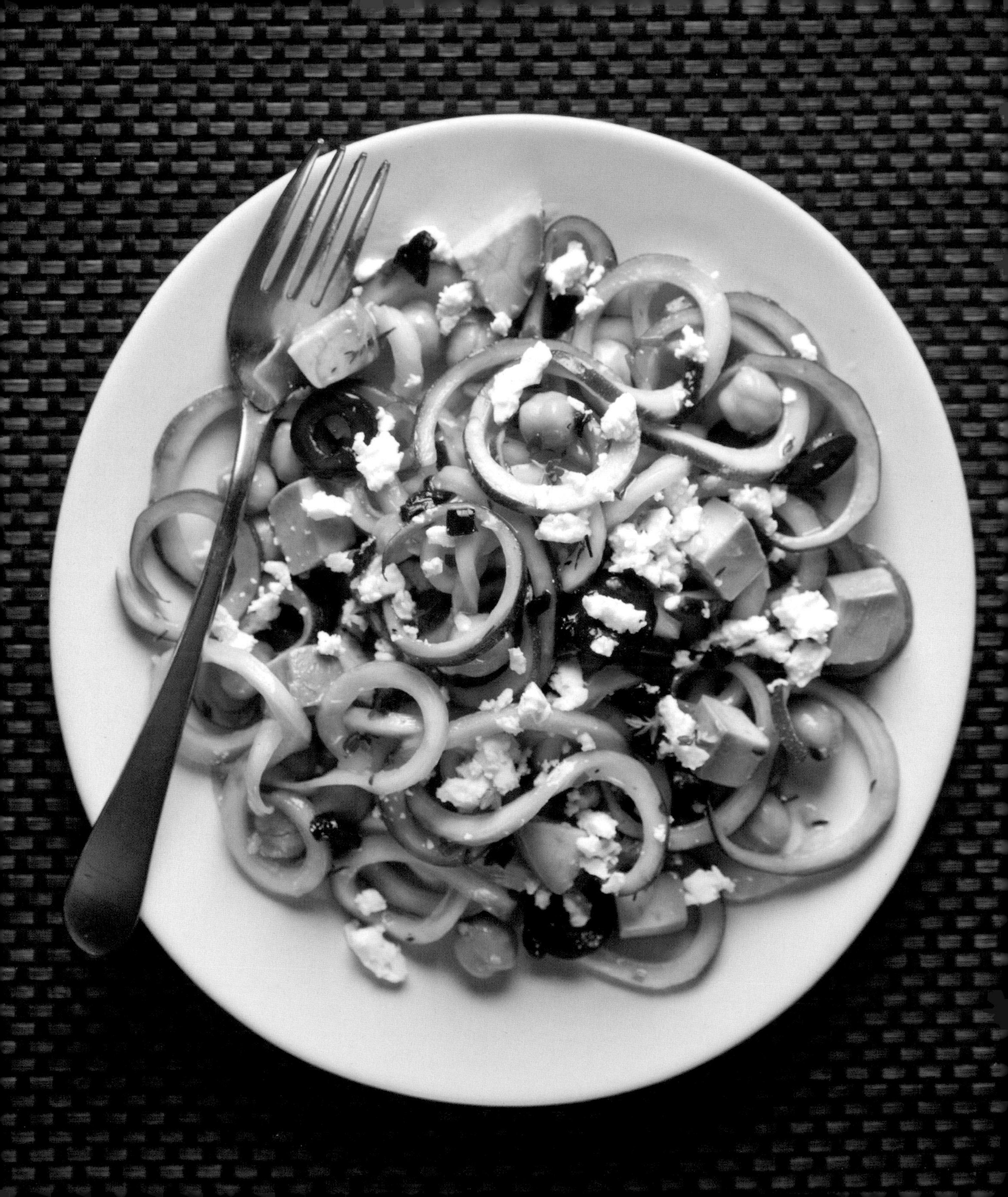

SALADS

ZESTY ZUCCHINI CHICKPEA SALAD

MAKES 6 SERVINGS

- 3 medium zucchini
- ½ teaspoon salt
- 5 tablespoons white vinegar
- 1 clove garlic, minced
- ¼ teaspoon dried thyme
- ½ cup extra virgin olive oil
- 1 cup cooked chickpeas
- ½ cup sliced pitted black olives
- 3 green onions, minced
- 1 canned chipotle pepper in adobo sauce, seeded and minced
- 1 ripe avocado
- ⅓ cup crumbled feta cheese

1. Cut zucchini into ribbons with thick spiral blade of spiralizer; cut into desired lengths. Place in medium bowl; sprinkle with salt. Toss to mix. Spread zucchini on several layers of paper towels. Let stand at room temperature 30 minutes to drain.

2. Combine vinegar, garlic and thyme in large bowl. Gradually whisk in oil until dressing is thoroughly blended. Pat zucchini dry; add to dressing. Add chickpeas, olives and green onions; toss lightly to coat. Cover; refrigerate at least 30 minutes or up to 4 hours, stirring occasionally.

3. Stir in chipotle pepper just before serving. Cut avocado into ½-inch cubes. Add avocado and cheese to salad; toss lightly to mix.

TIP: If you don't have a spiralizer, halve the zucchini lengthwise and then cut into ¼-inch slices.

GREEK SALAD WITH MARINATED TOFU

MAKES 4 TO 6 SERVINGS

MARINATED TOFU

- 1 package (14 ounces) firm or extra firm tofu
- ½ cup extra virgin olive oil
- ¼ cup fresh lemon juice
- 2 teaspoons salt
- 2 teaspoons dried Greek or Italian seasoning
- ½ teaspoon black pepper
- 1 teaspoon onion powder
- ½ teaspoon garlic powder

SALAD

- 1 pint grape tomatoes, halved
- 2 seedless cucumbers, quartered lengthwise and sliced
- 1 yellow bell pepper, slivered
- 1 small red onion, thinly sliced

1. Cut tofu crosswise into two pieces, each about 1 inch thick. Place on cutting board lined with paper towels; top with layer of paper towels. Place weighted baking dish on top of tofu. Let stand 30 minutes to drain. Pat tofu dry and crumble into large bowl.

2. Combine oil, lemon juice, salt, Greek seasoning and black pepper in small jar with lid; shake until well blended. Reserve ¼ cup mixture for salad dressing. Add onion powder and garlic powder to remaining mixture; pour over tofu and toss gently. Cover and refrigerate 2 hours or overnight.

3. For salad, combine tomatoes, cucumbers, bell pepper and onion in serving bowl. Add tofu and reserved dressing. Toss gently.

TIP: Marinating tofu is a great way to experience creamy, tangy feta for those who have a dairy sensitivity or just wish to avoid cheese and saturated fat. If you prefer, you can substitute 8 ounces of feta cheese for the tofu; proceed to step 2.

GREEK-STYLE CUCUMBER SALAD

MAKES 4 SERVINGS

1 medium cucumber, peeled and diced

¼ cup chopped green onions

1 teaspoon minced fresh dill

1 clove garlic, minced

1 cup sour cream

½ teaspoon salt

¼ teaspoon black pepper

⅛ teaspoon ground cumin

Fresh lemon juice (optional)

1. Place cucumber, green onions, dill and garlic in medium bowl.

2. Combine sour cream, salt, pepper and cumin in small bowl; stir until blended. Stir into cucumber mixture. Sprinkle with lemon juice to taste, if desired.

MAIN-DISH
MEDITERRANEAN SALAD

MAKES 4 SERVINGS

1   package (10 ounces) chopped
    romaine lettuce

8   ounces fresh green beans,
    cooked and drained

1   package (5½ ounces) solid white
    tuna, flaked

8   ounces cherry tomatoes, halved

2   tablespoons extra virgin olive oil

2   tablespoons cider vinegar or
    white vinegar

1½ teaspoons Dijon mustard

½   teaspoon black pepper

¼   teaspoon salt

1. Place lettuce, green beans, tuna and tomatoes in large bowl.

2. To make dressing, whisk oil, vinegar, mustard, pepper and salt in small bowl until blended. Pour dressing over salad; toss well. Serve immediately.

FRENCH LENTIL SALAD

MAKES 4 SERVINGS

1½ cups **dried lentils, rinsed and sorted**

4 **green onions, finely chopped**

3 **tablespoons balsamic vinegar**

2 **tablespoons chopped fresh parsley**

1 **tablespoon extra virgin olive oil**

½ **teaspoon salt**

½ **teaspoon dried thyme**

¼ **teaspoon black pepper**

Lettuce leaves (optional)

¼ **cup chopped walnuts, toasted***

*To toast walnuts, spread in single layer in heavy skillet. Cook over medium heat 1 to 2 minutes, stirring frequently until lightly browned. Remove from skillet immediately. Cool before using.

1. Combine 2 quarts water and lentils in large saucepan; bring to a boil over high heat. Reduce heat to low; cover and simmer 30 minutes or until lentils are tender, stirring occasionally. Drain lentils.

2. Combine cooked lentils, green onions, vinegar, parsley, oil, salt, thyme and pepper in large bowl; mix well. Cover and refrigerate 1 hour or until cool.

3. Serve on lettuce leaves, if desired. Top with toasted walnuts before serving.

MEDITERRANEAN CHICKEN SALAD

¼ **cup Italian Salad Dressing (page 51)**

4 **cups spring salad greens or mesclun**

1 **cup diced or shredded cooked chicken**

2 **plum tomatoes, sliced**

½ **cup croutons**

¼ **cup chopped fresh basil**

   Black pepper (optional)

1. Prepare dressing.

2. Combine greens, chicken, tomatoes, croutons, basil and dressing in large bowl; toss well.

3. Transfer mixture to plates. Season with pepper, if desired.

ITALIAN SALAD DRESSING
MAKES ⅔ CUP

3 tablespoons white or red wine vinegar

1 teaspoon minced garlic

1 teaspoon honey

1 teaspoon Dijon mustard

½ teaspoon salt

½ teaspoon onion powder

¼ teaspoon dried basil

¼ teaspoon dried oregano

   Pinch red pepper flakes

   Black pepper

¼ cup vegetable oil

¼ cup extra virgin olive oil

1. Combine vinegar, garlic, honey, mustard, salt, onion powder, basil, oregano, red pepper flakes and black pepper in small bowl.

2. Whisk in vegetable oil and olive oil in thin steady stream until well blended. Or combine all ingredients in jar with tight-fitting lid; cover jar and shake until well blended. Store in refrigerator.

GREEK LENTIL SALAD WITH FETA VINAIGRETTE

MAKES 3 SERVINGS

4 cups water

¾ cup uncooked lentils, rinsed and sorted

1 teaspoon salt, divided

1 bay leaf

¼ cup chopped green onions

1 stalk celery, chopped

1 cup grape tomatoes, halved

¼ cup crumbled feta cheese

2 tablespoons extra virgin olive oil

1 tablespoon white wine vinegar

½ teaspoon dried thyme

½ teaspoon dried oregano

¼ teaspoon black pepper

1. Combine water, lentils, ½ teaspoon salt and bay leaf in small saucepan. Bring to a boil. Reduce heat to medium-low; partially cover and cook 40 minutes or until lentils are tender but not mushy.

2. Drain lentils; remove and discard bay leaf. Place lentils in serving bowl; stir in green onions, celery and tomatoes.

3. Combine feta, oil, vinegar, thyme, oregano, remaining ½ teaspoon salt and pepper in small bowl. Pour over salad; gently stir until blended. Let stand at least 10 minutes before serving to allow flavors to blend.

MIDDLE EASTERN SPINACH SALAD

MAKES 4 SERVINGS

¼ **cup fresh lemon juice**

 1 **tablespoon packed brown sugar**

 1 **tablespoon extra virgin olive oil**

½ **teaspoon curry powder**

 1 **pound fresh spinach**

½ **cup golden raisins**

¼ **cup minced red onion**

¼ **cup thin red onion slices**

1. For dressing, whisk lemon juice, brown sugar, oil and curry powder in small bowl until blended.

2. Wash spinach well to remove sand and grit; remove stems and bruised leaves. Drain well; pat dry with paper towels. Tear spinach into bite-size pieces.

3. Toss spinach, raisins, minced onion and onion slices in large bowl. Add dressing; toss gently to coat.

GREEK CHICKPEA SALAD

MAKES 4 SERVINGS

4 cups packed baby spinach leaves

1 cup cooked chickpeas

1 large shallot, thinly sliced

4 pitted kalamata olives, sliced

2 tablespoons crumbled feta
   cheese

¼ cup plain Greek yogurt

2 teaspoons white wine vinegar

1 clove garlic, minced

1 teaspoon extra virgin olive oil

¼ teaspoon salt

¼ teaspoon black pepper

1. Combine spinach, chickpeas, shallot, olives and feta cheese in large bowl; toss gently.

2. Whisk yogurt, vinegar, garlic, oil, salt and pepper in small bowl until well blended. Add to salad; toss gently.

FENNEL, OLIVE AND RADICCHIO SALAD

MAKES 4 SERVINGS

½ **cup Italian- or Greek-style black olives, divided**

¼ **cup extra virgin olive oil**

1 **tablespoon lemon juice**

1 **flat anchovy fillet** *or* **½ teaspoon anchovy paste**

¼ **teaspoon salt**

Dash black pepper

Pinch sugar

1 **bulb fennel**

1 **head radicchio***

Fennel tops (optional)

*Radicchio, a tart red chicory, is available in large supermarkets and specialty food shops. If it is not available, substitute 2 heads of Belgian endive. Although it does not provide the dramatic red color, it will provide a similar texture, and its slightly bitter flavor will go well with the robust dressing and the sweet anise flavor of fennel.

1. For dressing, cut 3 olives in half; remove and discard pits. Place pitted olives, oil, lemon juice and anchovy in food processor or blender; process 5 seconds. Add salt, pepper and sugar; process about 5 seconds or until olives are finely chopped. Set aside.

2. Cut off and discard fennel stalks, reserving green leafy tops for garnish. Cut off and discard root end and any discolored parts of bulb. Cut bulb lengthwise into 8 wedges; separate each wedge into segments.

3. Separate radicchio leaves; rinse thoroughly. Drain well.

4. Arrange radicchio leaves, fennel and remaining olives on serving plate. Spoon dressing over salad; garnish with fennel leaves. Serve immediately.

VEGETABLES

SPINACH AND FARRO STUFFED PEPPERS

MAKES 6 SERVINGS

1 package (about 8 ounces) quick-cooking farro

1 tablespoon olive oil

½ cup sliced green onions

1 package (5 ounces) baby spinach

2 cloves garlic, crushed

1 tablespoon chopped fresh oregano

1 can (about 14 ounces) petite diced tomatoes, drained

½ teaspoon salt

⅛ teaspoon black pepper

1 container (4 ounces) crumbled feta cheese, divided

3 large bell peppers, halved lengthwise, cores and ribs removed

1. Preheat oven to 350°F. Prepare farro according to package directions using vegetable broth instead of water, if desired.

2. Heat oil in large skillet over medium-high heat. Add green onions, spinach, garlic and oregano; cook and stir 3 minutes. Stir in farro, tomatoes, salt, black pepper and ½ cup cheese.

3. Spoon farro mixture into bell pepper halves (about ¾ cup each); place in shallow baking pan. Pour ¼ cup water into bottom of pan; cover with foil.

4. Bake 30 minutes or until bell peppers are crisp-tender and filling is heated through. Sprinkle with remaining cheese.

SLOW-COOKED SHAKSHUKA

MAKES 6 SERVINGS

PREP TIME: 15 MINUTES
COOK TIME: 3 HOURS 15 MINUTES

- ¼ **cup extra virgin olive oil**
- 1 **medium onion, chopped**
- 1 **large red bell pepper, chopped**
- 3 **cloves garlic, sliced**
- 1 **can (28 ounces) crushed tomatoes with basil, garlic and oregano**
- 2 **teaspoons paprika**
- 2 **teaspoons ground cumin**
- 2 **teaspoons sugar**
- ½ **teaspoon salt**
- ¼ **teaspoon red pepper flakes**
- ¾ **cup crumbled feta cheese**
- 6 **eggs**
  Finely chopped fresh cilantro or parsley (optional)

SLOW COOKER DIRECTIONS

1. Coat inside of slow cooker with nonstick cooking spray. Combine oil, onion, bell pepper, garlic, tomatoes, paprika, cumin, sugar, salt and red pepper flakes in slow cooker. Cover; cook on HIGH 3 hours.

2. Stir in feta cheese. Make 6 indentations in tomato mixture; crack 1 egg into each indentation.

3. Cover; cook on HIGH 15 to 18 minutes or until egg whites are set but yolks are still creamy. Scoop eggs and sauce into serving dishes. Sprinkle with cilantro.

POTATO GNOCCHI WITH TOMATO SAUCE

2 pounds baking potatoes (3 or 4 large)

Tomato Sauce (page 63)

⅔ to 1 cup all-purpose flour, divided

1 egg yolk

½ teaspoon salt

⅛ teaspoon ground nutmeg (optional)

Grated Parmesan cheese

Slivered fresh basil

1. Preheat oven to 425°F. Pierce potatoes several times with fork. Bake 1 hour or until soft. Meanwhile, prepare Tomato Sauce.

2. Cut potatoes in half lengthwise; cool slightly. Scoop out potatoes from skins into medium bowl; discard skins. Mash potatoes until smooth. Add ⅓ cup flour, egg yolk, salt and nutmeg, if desired; mix well to form dough.

3. Turn out dough onto well-floured surface. Knead in enough remaining flour to form smooth dough. Divide dough into four pieces; roll each into ¾- to 1-inch-wide rope. Cut each rope into 1-inch pieces; gently press thumb into center of each piece to make indentation or roll over tines of fork. Place finished gnocchi on lightly floured kitchen towel in single layer to prevent sticking.

4. Bring 4 quarts salted water to a boil in large saucepan over high heat. To test cooking time, drop several gnocchi into water; cook 1 minute or until they float to surface. Remove from water with slotted spoon and taste for doneness. (If gnocchi start to dissolve, shorten cooking time by several seconds.) Cook remaining gnocchi in batches, removing with slotted spoon to warm serving dish.

5. Serve gnocchi with sauce; sprinkle with cheese and basil.

TOMATO SAUCE
MAKES ABOUT 2 CUPS

2 tablespoons olive oil or butter

1 clove garlic, minced

1 can (28 ounces) Italian plum tomatoes, chopped, juice reserved

1 teaspoon sugar

1 tablespoon chopped fresh basil

Salt and black pepper

1. Heat oil in medium saucepan over medium heat. Add garlic; cook 30 seconds or until fragrant. Stir in tomatoes with juice and sugar; cook 20 minutes.

2. Stir in basil; cook 2 minutes. Season to taste with salt and pepper.

TIP: When plum tomatoes are in season, substitute fresh tomatoes for canned. Use 2 pounds peeled, seeded and chopped tomatoes, and decrease cooking time to 10 minutes.

EGGPLANT CRÊPES WITH ROASTED TOMATO SAUCE

MAKES 4 TO 6 SERVINGS

Roasted Tomato Sauce (page 65)

2 eggplants, cut into 18 (¼-inch-thick) slices

Olive oil

1 package (10 ounces) frozen chopped spinach, thawed and squeezed dry

1 cup ricotta cheese

½ cup grated Parmesan cheese

1¼ cups (5 ounces) shredded Gruyère or Swiss cheese

1. Prepare Roasted Tomato Sauce. *Reduce oven temperature to 425°F.*

2. Arrange eggplant on baking sheets in single layer. Brush both sides of eggplant slices with oil. Bake 10 minutes; turn and bake 5 to 10 minutes or until tender. Cool. *Reduce oven temperature to 350°F.*

3. Spray 12×8-inch baking dish with nonstick cooking spray. Combine spinach, ricotta and Parmesan cheeses; mix well. Spread spinach mixture evenly on eggplant slices; roll up slices, beginning at short ends. Place rolls, seam-side down, in baking dish.

4. Cover dish with foil. Bake 25 minutes. Uncover; sprinkle rolls with Gruyère cheese. Bake, uncovered, 5 minutes or until cheese is melted. Serve with sauce.

ROASTED TOMATO SAUCE
MAKES ABOUT 1 CUP

3 pounds ripe plum tomatoes
(about 20), cut in half and
seeded

3 tablespoons olive oil, divided

½ teaspoon salt

⅓ cup minced fresh basil

½ teaspoon black pepper

1. Preheat oven to 450°F. Toss tomatoes with
1 tablespoon oil and salt. Place cut sides down on baking
sheet.

2. Bake 20 to 25 minutes or until skins are blistered.
Cool. Process tomatoes, remaining 2 tablespoons oil, basil
and pepper in food processor until smooth.

ROASTED MUSHROOMS WITH SHALLOTS

MAKES 4 SERVINGS

1 **pound cremini mushrooms, halved**

½ **cup sliced shallots**

1 **tablespoon olive oil**

½ **teaspoon kosher salt**

½ **teaspoon dried rosemary**

¼ **teaspoon black pepper**

1. Preheat oven to 400°F.

2. Spread mushrooms and shallots on rimmed baking sheet. Whisk oil, salt, rosemary and pepper in small bowl. Pour over mushrooms and shallots; toss to coat evenly. Spread in single layer.

3. Bake 15 to 18 minutes or until mushrooms are browned and tender.

ZUCCHINI WITH TOASTED CHICKPEA FLOUR

MAKES 4 SERVINGS

½ cup sifted chickpea flour

3 tablespoons olive oil

3 teaspoons minced garlic

2 zucchini, halved lengthwise then cut into ½-inch-thick slices

2 summer squash, halved lengthwise then cut into ½-inch-thick slices

1 teaspoon salt

½ teaspoon black pepper

½ cup water

1. Heat large skillet over medium-high heat; add chickpea flour. Cook and stir 3 to 4 minutes until fragrant and slightly darker in color. Remove from skillet; set aside.

2. Heat oil in same skillet over medium-high heat. Add garlic; cook and stir 1 minute or until fragrant. Add zucchini, squash, salt and pepper; cook and stir 5 minutes or until beginning to soften.

3. Stir chickpea flour into skillet to coat vegetables. Pour in water; cook and stir 2 to 3 minutes or until moist crumbs form, scraping bottom of skillet frequently to prevent sticking and scrape up brown bits.

SPAGHETTI SQUASH WITH CHUNKY TOMATO SAUCE

1 spaghetti squash (about 4 pounds)

1 tablespoon olive oil

2 cups (6 ounces) sliced cremini mushrooms

½ cup diced onion

½ cup diced green bell pepper

1 can (about 14 ounces) diced tomatoes

½ cup tomato sauce

⅓ cup water

½ teaspoon dried oregano

¼ teaspoon salt

⅛ teaspoon black pepper

4 (3-ounce) cooked chicken sausage links, cut into pieces

2 tablespoons chopped fresh Italian parsley

1. Cut spaghetti squash lengthwise in half. Remove seeds. Place squash in 12×8-inch microwavable dish. Cover with vented plastic wrap. Microwave on HIGH 9 minutes or until squash separates easily into strands when tested with fork. Cut each squash half lengthwise in half; separate strands with fork.

2. Heat oil in large skillet over medium-high heat. Add mushrooms, onion and bell pepper; cook and stir 7 minutes or until vegetables are tender.

3. Stir tomatoes, tomato sauce, water, oregano, salt and black pepper into skillet. Bring to a simmer. Reduce heat; cover and cook 5 minutes. Stir in sausage pieces.

4. Place squash on serving plates. Top with sauce and sprinkle with parsley.

EGGPLANT PARMESAN

MAKES 12 SERVINGS

- 2 **eggs**
- 1 **teaspoon dried basil**
- ½ **teaspoon salt**
- ¼ **teaspoon black pepper**
- 1½ **cups panko or plain dry bread crumbs**
- ½ **cup plus 2 tablespoons grated Parmesan cheese, divided**
- 2 **medium eggplants (1 pound each), cut lengthwise into ¾-inch slices**
- 2 **cups vegetable oil**
- 1 **cup ricotta cheese**
- 2 **cups (8 ounces) shredded mozzarella cheese**
- 1 **can (about 28 ounces) tomato sauce or Tomato Sauce (page 63)**

1. Preheat oven to 350°F. Spray 13×9-inch baking pan with nonstick cooking spray.

2. Whisk eggs, basil, salt and pepper in shallow dish until blended. Combine panko and ½ cup Parmesan cheese in another shallow dish. Dip eggplant in egg mixture, letting excess drip back into bowl. Coat both sides with crumb mixture.

3. Heat oil in large skillet. Cook eggplant in batches 2 minutes per side or until golden. Drain on paper towel-lined plate.

4. Combine ricotta cheese and mozzarella cheese in small bowl. Place one third of eggplant in bottom of prepared pan. Spread scant 1 cup tomato sauce over eggplant. Top with half of cheese mixture; repeat layers, ending with sauce. Bake 30 minutes or until eggplant is fork-tender and cheese is melted.

5. Preheat broiler. Sprinkle remaining 2 tablespoons Parmesan cheese over eggplant. Broil 6 inches from heat 3 minutes or until cheese is browned. Let stand 10 minutes before serving.

ARTICHOKES WITH LEMON-TARRAGON BUTTER

MAKES 2 SERVINGS

6 cups water

2¼ teaspoons salt, divided

2 whole artichokes, stems cut off and leaf tips trimmed

¼ cup (½ stick) butter

¼ teaspoon grated lemon peel

2 tablespoons fresh lemon juice

¼ teaspoon dried tarragon

1. Bring water and 2 teaspoons salt to a boil in large saucepan over high heat. Add artichokes; return to a boil. Reduce heat to medium-low; cover and simmer 35 to 45 minutes or until leaves detach easily.

2. Turn artichokes upside down to drain well. Cut artichokes in half and remove the fuzzy choke at the bottom that covers the artichoke heart with a spoon.

3. Combine butter, lemon peel, lemon juice, tarragon and remaining ¼ teaspoon salt in small saucepan; heat over low heat until butter is melted. Serve in small bowls for dipping.

ZOODLES IN TOMATO SAUCE

MAKES 4 SERVINGS

- 3 teaspoons olive oil, divided
- 2 cloves garlic
- 1 tablespoon tomato paste
- 1 can (28 ounces) whole tomatoes
- 1 teaspoon dried oregano
- ½ teaspoon salt
- 2 large zucchini (about 16 ounces each), ends trimmed, cut into 3-inch pieces
- ¼ cup shredded Parmesan cheese

1. Heat 2 teaspoons oil in medium saucepan over medium heat. Add garlic; cook 1 minute or until fragrant but not browned. Stir in tomato paste; cook 30 seconds, stirring constantly. Add tomatoes with juice, oregano and salt; break up tomatoes with wooden spoon. Bring to a simmer. Reduce heat; cook 30 minutes or until thickened.

2. Meanwhile, cut zucchini into ribbons with fine spiral blade of spiralizer. Heat remaining 1 teaspoon oil in large skillet over medium-high heat. Add zucchini; cook 4 to 5 minutes or until tender, stirring frequently. Transfer to serving plates; top with tomato sauce and Parmesan cheese.

TIP: If you don't have a spiralizer, cut the zucchini into ribbons with a mandoline or sharp knife. Or cut it into small wedges to mimic a small pasta shape. Cut it lengthwise into quarters and then thinly slice it crosswise.

MEAT AND POULTRY

CHICKEN CASSOULET

MAKES 6 SERVINGS

4 slices bacon

¼ cup all-purpose flour
Salt and black pepper

1¾ pounds bone-in chicken pieces

2 chicken sausages (2¼ ounces each), cooked and cut into ¼-inch pieces

1 medium onion, chopped

1½ cups diced red and green bell peppers

2 cloves garlic, minced

1 teaspoon dried thyme

1 teaspoon olive oil

½ cup dry white wine

2 cans (about 15 ounces each) cannellini or Great Northern beans, rinsed and drained

1. Preheat oven to 350°F.

2. Cook bacon in Dutch oven over medium-high heat until crisp; drain on paper towels. Cut into 1-inch pieces. Pour off all but 2 tablespoons drippings.

3. Place flour in shallow bowl; season with salt and black pepper. Dip chicken pieces in flour mixture; shake off excess. Brown chicken in batches in Dutch oven over medium-high heat; transfer to plate. Lightly brown sausages in same Dutch oven; transfer to plate.

4. Add onion, bell peppers, garlic and thyme to Dutch oven; cook and stir over medium heat 5 minutes or until softened, adding oil as needed to prevent sticking. Add wine; cook and stir over medium heat, scraping up browned bits from bottom of pan. Add beans; mix well. Top with chicken, sausages and bacon.

5. Cover and bake 40 minutes. Remove cover; bake 15 minutes or until chicken is cooked through (165°F).

BROILED TURKEY TENDERLOIN KABOBS

¼ cup orange juice

2 tablespoons soy sauce, divided

1 clove garlic, minced

1 teaspoon fresh grated ginger

12 ounces turkey tenderloin (about 2 medium), cut into 1-inch cubes

1 tablespoon molasses

1 green bell pepper, cut into 1-inch pieces

1 red onion, cut into 1½-inch pieces

Hot cooked brown rice

1. Combine orange juice, 1 tablespoon soy sauce, garlic and ginger in large bowl. Pour half of mixture into small bowl; cover and refrigerate. Add turkey to remaining mixture; stir to coat. Cover and marinate in refrigerator 2 hours, stirring occasionally.

2. For glaze, whisk remaining 1 tablespoon soy sauce and molasses into reserved marinade mixture.

3. Line baking sheet with foil; spray with nonstick cooking spray. Remove turkey from marinade; discard marinade.

4. Alternately thread turkey, bell pepper and onion onto 4 skewers.* Place on prepared baking sheet.

5. Broil 4 inches from heat source 3 minutes. Brush evenly with glaze. Broil 6 to 9 minutes or until turkey is no longer pink. Serve skewers on rice.

*Soak wooden skewers in warm water 20 minutes to prevent burning.

HONEY LEMON GARLIC CHICKEN

MAKES 4 SERVINGS

2 lemons, divided

2 tablespoons olive oil

2 tablespoons honey

3 cloves garlic, chopped

2 fresh rosemary sprigs, leaves removed from stems

1 teaspoon coarse salt

½ teaspoon black pepper

3 pounds bone-in skin-on chicken thighs and drumsticks

1¼ pounds unpeeled small potatoes, cut into halves or quarters

1. Preheat oven to 375°F. Grate peel and squeeze juice from 1 lemon. Slice remaining lemon.

2. Combine lemon peel, lemon juice, oil, honey, garlic, rosemary leaves, salt and pepper in small bowl; mix well. Combine chicken, potatoes and lemon slices in large bowl. Pour oil mixture over chicken and potatoes; toss to coat. Arrange in single layer on large rimmed baking sheet or in shallow roasting pan.

3. Bake about 1 hour or until potatoes are tender and chicken is cooked through (165°F). Cover loosely with foil if chicken skin is becoming too dark.

POMEGRANATE CHICKEN WINGS

MAKES 6 SERVINGS

4 **cups pomegranate juice**

2 **cups walnuts, toasted***

1 **tablespoon vegetable oil**

1 **large onion, finely diced**

3 **pounds chicken wings, tips removed and split at joints**

2 **tablespoons sugar**

1¼ **teaspoons kosher salt**

¼ **teaspoon ground cinnamon**

¼ **teaspoon black pepper**

Hot cooked basmati rice or pearled couscous

Pomegranate seeds and chopped fresh parsley (optional)

*To toast walnuts, spread in single layer in heavy skillet. Cook and stir 1 to 2 minutes over medium heat until nuts are lightly browned. Immediately remove from skillet.

SLOW COOKER DIRECTIONS

1. Pour pomegranate juice into small saucepan; bring to a boil over high heat. Boil 18 to 20 minutes or until juice is reduced to 2 cups.

2. Meanwhile, place walnuts in food processor; pulse until finely ground. Place in slow cooker.

3. Heat oil in large skillet over medium-high heat. Add onion; cook and stir 6 minutes or until translucent. Add wings, pomegranate juice, sugar, salt, cinnamon and pepper to slow cooker.

4. Cover; cook on HIGH 3 to 4 hours. Serve over rice; garnish with pomegranate seeds and parsley.

SPICED CHICKEN SKEWERS WITH YOGURT-TAHINI SAUCE

MAKES 8 SERVINGS

1 cup plain Greek yogurt

¼ cup chopped fresh parsley, plus additional for garnish

¼ cup tahini

2 tablespoons fresh lemon juice

1 clove garlic

¾ teaspoon salt, divided

1 tablespoon olive oil

2 teaspoons garam masala

1 pound boneless skinless chicken breasts, cut into 1-inch pieces

1. Spray grid of grill with nonstick cooking spray. Prepare grill for direct cooking.

2. For sauce, combine yogurt, ¼ cup parsley, tahini, lemon juice, garlic and ¼ teaspoon salt in food processor or blender; process until combined. Set aside.

3. Combine oil, garam masala and remaining ½ teaspoon salt in medium bowl. Add chicken; toss to coat evenly. Thread chicken on 8 (6-inch) metal or wooden skewers.*

4. Grill skewers over medium-high heat 5 minutes per side or until chicken is no longer pink. Serve with sauce. Garnish with additional parsley.

*Soak wooden skewers in warm water 20 minutes to prevent burning.

FORTY-CLOVE CHICKEN FILICE

1 whole chicken (about 3 pounds), cut into serving pieces

Salt and black pepper

¼ cup olive oil

40 cloves garlic (about 2 heads), peeled

4 stalks celery, thickly sliced

½ cup dry white wine

¼ cup dry vermouth*

Grated peel and juice of 1 lemon

2 tablespoons finely chopped fresh parsley

2 teaspoons dried basil

1 teaspoon dried oregano

Pinch of red pepper flakes

Or substitute chicken broth or additional white wine.

1. Preheat oven to 375°F.

2. Season chicken with salt and black pepper. Heat oil in Dutch oven. Add chicken; cook until browned on all sides.

3. Combine garlic, celery, wine, vermouth, lemon juice, parsley, basil, oregano and red pepper flakes in medium bowl; pour over chicken. Sprinkle with lemon peel; season with additional salt and black pepper.

4. Cover and bake 40 minutes. Remove cover; bake 15 minutes or until chicken is cooked through (165°F).

MARINATED BEEF BROCHETTES

MAKES 6 SERVINGS

¼ cup finely chopped onion

¼ cup olive oil

3 tablespoons fresh lime juice

1 finely chopped seeded hot finger pepper (about 1 teaspoon)

1 clove garlic, minced

12 ounces beef tenderloin, cut into 1-inch cubes

1 green bell pepper, cut into 1-inch pieces

1 red onion, cut into 1-inch pieces

1. Combine chopped onion, oil, lime juice, hot pepper and garlic in medium bowl; mix well. Combine beef and marinade in large resealable food storage bag. Seal bag; turn to coat. Refrigerate 2 hours or overnight.

2. Prepare grill for direct cooking. Remove beef from marinade; discard marinade. Alternately thread beef, bell pepper and red onion pieces onto six 8-inch wooden skewers.*

3. Grill skewers 2 to 3 minutes per side or until desired doneness.

Soak wooden skewers in warm water 20 minutes to prevent burning.

CHORIZO AND ARTICHOKE KABOBS WITH MUSTARD VINAIGRETTE

MAKES 6 SERVINGS

1 can (about 14 ounces) large artichoke hearts, drained

2 (3-ounce) fully cooked chorizo-flavored chicken sausages or andouille sausages

3 tablespoons olive oil

2 teaspoons white wine vinegar

1 teaspoon Dijon mustard
  Salt and black pepper

1. Preheat broiler. Line baking sheet or broiler pan with heavy-duty foil.

2. Cut artichokes in half. Cut each sausage diagonally into 6 slices. Arrange 2 artichoke pieces and 2 sausage slices on each of 6 wooden skewers.* Place skewers on prepared baking sheet. Broil 4 inches from heat 4 minutes or until artichokes are hot and sausage is browned.

3. Meanwhile, whisk oil, vinegar and mustard in small bowl. Season with salt and pepper. Serve with kabobs.

*Soak wooden skewers in warm water 20 minutes to prevent burning.

PROVENÇAL LEMON AND OLIVE CHICKEN

MAKES 8 SERVINGS

PREP TIME: 15 MINUTES
COOK TIME: 5 TO 6 HOURS (LOW) OR
3 TO 3½ HOURS (HIGH)

- 2 cups chopped onions
- 8 skinless chicken thighs (about 2½ pounds)
- 1 lemon, thinly sliced and seeded
- 1 cup pitted green olives
- 1 tablespoon olive brine or white wine vinegar
- 2 teaspoons herbes de Provence
- 1 bay leaf
- ½ teaspoon salt
- ⅛ teaspoon black pepper
- 1 cup chicken broth
- ½ cup minced fresh Italian parsley

  Hot cooked rice or orzo

SLOW COOKER DIRECTIONS

1. Place onions in slow cooker. Arrange chicken and lemon slices over onion. Add olives, brine, herbes de Provence, bay leaf, salt and pepper. Pour in broth.

2. Cover; cook on LOW 5 to 6 hours or on HIGH 3 to 3½ hours or until chicken is tender. Remove and discard bay leaf. Stir in parsley; serve over rice.

GREEK LAMB WITH TZATZIKI SAUCE

MAKES 4 TO 6 SERVINGS

2½ to 3 pounds boneless leg of lamb

8 cloves garlic, divided

¼ cup Dijon mustard

2 tablespoons minced fresh rosemary leaves

2 teaspoons salt

2 teaspoons black pepper

¼ cup plus 2 teaspoons olive oil, divided

1 small seedless cucumber

1 tablespoon chopped fresh mint

1 teaspoon lemon juice

2 cups plain Greek yogurt

1. Untie and unroll lamb to lie flat; trim fat.

2. For marinade, mince 4 cloves garlic; place in small bowl. Add mustard, rosemary, salt and pepper; whisk in ¼ cup olive oil. Spread mixture evenly over lamb, coating both sides. Place lamb in large resealable food storage bag. Seal bag; refrigerate at least 2 hours or overnight, turning several times.

3. Meanwhile, prepare Tzatziki Sauce. Mince remaining 4 cloves garlic and mash to a paste; place in medium bowl. Peel and grate cucumber; squeeze to remove excess moisture. Add cucumber, mint, remaining 2 teaspoons olive oil and lemon juice to bowl with garlic. Add yogurt; mix well. Refrigerate until ready to serve.

4. Prepare grill for direct cooking. Grill lamb over medium-high heat 35 to 40 minutes or to desired doneness. Cover loosely with foil; let rest 5 to 10 minutes. (Remove from grill at 140°F for medium. Temperature will rise 5°F while resting.) Slice lamb and serve with sauce.

MEDITERRANEAN CHICKEN KABOBS OVER COUSCOUS

MAKES 8 SERVINGS

2 pounds boneless skinless chicken breasts or chicken tenders, cut into 1-inch pieces

1 small eggplant, peeled and cut into 1-inch pieces

1 medium zucchini, cut crosswise into ½-inch slices

2 medium onions, each cut into 8 wedges

16 medium mushrooms, stemmed

32 cherry tomatoes

1 cup chicken broth

⅔ cup balsamic vinegar

3 tablespoons olive oil

2 tablespoons dried mint

4 teaspoons dried basil

1 tablespoon dried oregano

2 teaspoons grated lemon peel

Chopped fresh parsley

4 cups hot cooked couscous

1. Alternately thread chicken, eggplant, zucchini, onions, mushrooms and tomatoes onto 16 metal or wooden skewers*; place in large glass baking dish.

2. Combine broth, vinegar, oil, mint, basil and oregano in small bowl; pour over kabobs. Cover; marinate in refrigerator 2 hours, turning occasionally. Remove kabobs from marinade; discard marinade.

3. Preheat broiler. Broil kabobs 6 inches from heat 10 to 15 minutes or until chicken is cooked through, turning kabobs halfway through cooking time.

4. Stir lemon peel and parsley into couscous; serve with kabobs.

*Soak wooden skewers in warm water 20 minutes to prevent burning.

TIP: These kabobs can be grilled instead of broiled. Spray the grill grid with nonstick cooking spray, then prepare the grill for direct cooking. Grill the kabobs, covered, over medium-hot coals 10 to 15 minutes or until the chicken is cooked through, turning kabobs once.

FISH AND SEAFOOD

LEMON ROSEMARY SHRIMP AND VEGETABLE SOUVLAKI

MAKES 4 KABOBS

8 ounces large raw shrimp, peeled and deveined (with tails on)

1 medium zucchini, halved lengthwise and cut into ½-inch slices

½ medium red bell pepper, cut into 1-inch pieces

8 green onions, trimmed and cut into 2-inch pieces

1 tablespoon extra virgin olive oil

SAUCE

3 tablespoons extra virgin olive oil

2 tablespoons fresh lemon juice

2 teaspoons grated lemon peel

2 cloves garlic, minced

½ teaspoon salt

½ teaspoon minced fresh rosemary

⅛ teaspoon red pepper flakes

1. Spray grid of grill or grill pan with nonstick cooking spray. Prepare grill for direct cooking.

2. Spray 4 (12-inch) bamboo or metal skewers with cooking spray. Alternately thread shrimp, zucchini, bell pepper and green onions onto skewers. Brush skewers with 1 tablespoon oil.

3. For sauce, combine 3 tablespoons oil, lemon juice, lemon peel, garlic, salt, rosemary and red pepper flakes in small bowl; mix well.

4. Grill skewers over high heat 2 minutes per side. Remove to serving platter; drizzle with sauce.

HALIBUT PROVENÇAL

MAKES 4 SERVINGS

2 tablespoons olive oil, divided

2 cups thinly sliced and chopped fennel bulb

1 cup finely chopped onion

1 can (28 ounces) diced tomatoes

2 tablespoons minced orange peel

2 teaspoons herbes de Provence

4 (4-ounce) halibut steaks (½ inch thick)

¼ cup plain dry bread crumbs

1 tablespoon grated Parmesan cheese

2 cloves garlic, minced

1 teaspoon paprika

½ teaspoon black pepper

¼ teaspoon salt

Minced fresh basil or parsley (optional)

1. Heat 1 tablespoon oil in large skillet over medium heat. Add fennel and onion; cook and stir 5 minutes or until crisp-tender. Add tomatoes, orange peel and herbes de Provence; cook and stir 10 minutes.

2. Meanwhile, combine bread crumbs, cheese, garlic, paprika, pepper and salt in small bowl.

3. Place halibut over vegetables; drizzle with remaining 1 tablespoon oil. Sprinkle bread crumb mixture over fish. Cover and cook 5 to 6 minutes or until fish begins to flake when tested with fork. Garnish with basil.

TIP: For a golden, crispy topping, preheat broiler. Place skillet under broiler; broil 1 to 2 minutes or until bread crumb mixture is golden brown. Sprinkle fish with minced basil, if desired.

ROASTED ALMOND TILAPIA

MAKES 2 SERVINGS

2 tilapia or Boston scrod fillets (6 ounces each)

¼ teaspoon salt

1 tablespoon Dijon mustard

¼ cup all-purpose flour

2 tablespoons chopped almonds

Paprika (optional)

Lemon wedges

1. Preheat oven to 450°F. Place fish on small baking sheet; season with salt. Spread mustard over fish. Combine flour and almonds in small bowl; sprinkle over fish. Press lightly to adhere. Sprinkle with paprika, if desired.

2. Bake 8 to 10 minutes or until fish is opaque in center and begins to flake when tested with fork. Serve with lemon wedges, if desired.

PROSCIUTTO-WRAPPED SNAPPER

MAKES 4 SERVINGS

1 tablespoon plus 1 teaspoon olive oil, divided

2 cloves garlic, minced

4 skinless red snapper or halibut fillets (6 to 7 ounces each)

½ teaspoon salt

½ teaspoon black pepper

8 large fresh sage leaves

8 thin slices prosciutto (4 ounces)

¼ cup dry marsala wine

1. Preheat oven to 400°F.

2. Combine 1 tablespoon oil and garlic in small bowl; brush over fish. Sprinkle with salt and pepper. Lay 2 sage leaves on each fillet. Wrap 2 slices prosciutto around fish to enclose sage leaves; tuck in ends of prosciutto.

3. Heat remaining 1 teaspoon oil in large ovenproof skillet over medium-high heat. Add fish, sage side down; cook 3 to 4 minutes or until prosciutto is crisp. Carefully turn fish. Transfer skillet to oven; bake 8 to 10 minutes or until fish is opaque in center.

4. Transfer fish to serving plates; keep warm. Pour wine into skillet; cook over medium-high heat, stirring to scrape up any browned bits. Stir constantly 2 to 3 minutes or until mixture has reduced by half. Drizzle over fish.

FRESH GARLIC SHRIMP LINGUINE

MAKES 4 SERVINGS

6 ounces uncooked linguine

8 ounces raw shrimp, peeled and deveined

¼ cup grated Parmesan cheese

3 tablespoons olive oil

1 clove garlic, minced

½ teaspoon seafood seasoning

¼ cup finely chopped fresh parsley

¼ teaspoon salt

1. Bring large saucepan of salted water to a boil. Add pasta; cook 6 minutes. Add shrimp; cook 3 to 4 minutes or until shrimp are pink and opaque and pasta is desired tenderness. Drain, reserving ¼ cup cooking water.

2. Add cheese, oil, garlic and seafood seasoning; toss gently to coat. Drizzle in a bit of reserved cooking water to make sauce that coats pasta. Add parsley and salt; toss to combine.

TIP: If you use a different shape of pasta, check the cook time on the package and add the shrimp during the last 3 to 4 minutes of cooking. If you would prefer to cook the pasta and shrimp separately, cook the pasta to desired doneness and then remove it with tongs, a spider or a fine mesh strainer. Return water to a boil; cook shrimp until pink and opaque. Drain shrimp and return to saucepan with pasta.

GRILLED TUNA NIÇOISE WITH CITRUS MARINADE

Italian Salad Dressing (page 51)

CITRUS MARINADE

- ½ cup fresh lime juice
- ¼ cup vegetable oil
- 2 green onions, chopped
- 1 teaspoon dried tarragon
- ¼ teaspoon garlic powder
- ¼ teaspoon salt
- ¼ teaspoon black pepper

SALAD

- 1 tuna steak (about 1 pound)
- 2 cups fresh green beans
- 4 cups romaine lettuce leaves, washed and torn
- 8 small red potatoes, cooked and quartered
- 1 cup chopped seeded fresh tomato
- 4 hard-cooked eggs, chopped
  Sliced red onions
  Chopped black olives

1. Prepare dressing.

2. For marinade, whisk lime juice, oil, green onions, tarragon, garlic powder, salt and pepper in medium bowl. Place tuna in large resealable food storage bag; add marinade. Seal bag; turn to coat. Marinate in refrigerator 1 hour, turning occasionally.

3. Prepare grill for direct cooking. Drain tuna; discard marinade. Grill 8 to 10 minutes or until tuna begins to flake when tested with fork, turning once. (Or broil tuna 4 inches from heat, 8 to 10 minutes, turning once.) Slice tuna into ¼-inch-thick slices; set aside.

4. Bring 2 cups water to a boil in large saucepan over high heat. Add beans; cook 2 minutes. Drain; rinse under cold water.

5. Place lettuce on large serving platter. Arrange tuna, beans, potatoes, tomato, eggs, onions and olives on lettuce. Serve with dressing.

GARLIC CLAMS

MAKES 4 SERVINGS

2 **pounds littleneck clams**

2 **teaspoons olive oil**

2 **tablespoons finely chopped onion**

2 **tablespoons chopped garlic**

½ **cup dry white wine**

¼ **cup chopped red bell pepper**

2 **tablespoons fresh lemon juice**

1 **tablespoon chopped fresh parsley**

1. Discard any clams that remain open when tapped with fingers. Scrub clams with stiff brush under cold running water. Soak clams 20 minutes in mixture of ½ cup salt to 1 gallon water. Drain water; repeat two more times.

2. Heat oil in large saucepan over medium-high heat. Add onion and garlic; cook and stir about 3 minutes or until garlic is tender but not brown. Add clams, wine, bell pepper and lemon juice. Cover; simmer 3 to 10 minutes or until clams open. Transfer clams as they open to large bowl; cover. Discard any clams that do not open.

3. Increase heat to high. Add parsley; boil until liquid reduces to ¼ to ⅓ cup. Pour over clams; serve immediately.

GRILLED SWORDFISH SICILIAN STYLE

MAKES 4 TO 6 SERVINGS

3   tablespoons extra virgin olive oil

1   clove garlic, minced

2   tablespoons fresh lemon juice

¾   teaspoon salt

⅛   teaspoon black pepper

3   tablespoons capers, drained

1   tablespoon chopped fresh oregano or basil

1½   pounds swordfish steaks (¾ inch thick)

1. Oil grid of grill. Prepare grill for direct cooking.

2. For sauce, heat oil in small saucepan over low heat; add garlic. Cook 1 minute. Remove from heat; cool slightly. Whisk in lemon juice, salt and pepper until salt is dissolved. Stir in capers and oregano.

3. Grill fish over medium heat 7 to 8 minutes or until opaque, turning once. Serve fish with sauce.

TIP: Instead of marinating the raw swordfish steaks, use the marinade as a sauce for the grilled fish.

TUNA SICILIAN STYLE

MAKES 4 SERVINGS

¾ **cup extra virgin olive oil**

Juice of 2 lemons

4 **cloves garlic, minced**

1 **tablespoon chopped fresh rosemary** *or* **1½ teaspoons dried rosemary**

1 **tablespoon chopped fresh parsley**

¾ **teaspoon salt**

½ **teaspoon black pepper**

4 **fresh tuna steaks (½ inch thick)**

Lemon slices (optional)

Arugula or spinach

1. For basting sauce, combine oil, lemon juice, garlic, rosemary, parsley, salt and pepper in medium bowl. Prepare grill for direct cooking.*

2. Set aside half of basting sauce until ready to serve. Brush both sides of tuna with basting sauce; place on grid over medium-high heat. Grill tuna 4 minutes, basting generously with sauce. Turn and grill 4 to 6 minutes, or until desired degree of doneness, brushing frequently with sauce. Add lemon slices to grill for last few minutes, if desired.

3. Serve tuna on arugula with reserved basting sauce. Serve with grilled lemon slices.

Tuna may also be prepared on stovetop grill pan.

MEDITERRANEAN SHRIMP AND BEAN SALAD

MAKES 2 TO 4 SERVINGS

10 ounces large cooked shrimp, cut into bite-size pieces

1½ cups grape or cherry tomatoes, halved

1 large shallot, minced

¾ cup cooked chickpeas

¼ cup shredded fresh basil

¼ teaspoon paprika

¼ teaspoon salt

¼ teaspoon black pepper

⅛ teaspoon dried oregano

3 tablespoons tomato or vegetable juice

1 tablespoon white wine vinegar

1 tablespoon olive oil

1. Combine shrimp, tomatoes, shallot, chickpeas and basil in large bowl.

2. Combine paprika, salt, pepper and oregano in small bowl. Whisk in tomato juice, vinegar and oil until well blended. Pour over salad; toss gently to coat.

BASIL-LIME SCALLOPS

MAKES 4 SERVINGS

2 tablespoons chopped fresh basil

Juice of 1 lime

1 teaspoon soy sauce

2 teaspoons olive oil, divided

1 clove garlic, minced

⅛ teaspoon red pepper flakes

8 jumbo sea scallops (about 1 pound)

Mixed baby greens (optional)

Lime wedges (optional)

1. Whisk basil, lime juice, soy sauce, 1 teaspoon oil, garlic and red pepper flakes in shallow bowl until smooth and well blended. Add scallops; turn to coat evenly. Marinate in refrigerator 30 minutes.

2. Heat remaining 1 teaspoon oil in large nonstick skillet over medium-high heat. Cook scallops 3 minutes per side or until desired doneness is reached.

3. Serve scallops with mixed greens and lime wedges, if desired.

TIP: There are two types of scallops available: sea scallops and bay scallops. Sea scallops are more widely available, although they're less tender. Bay scallops are smaller, slightly sweeter and more expensive.

PASTA

GREEK PASTA SALAD

MAKES 6 TO 8 SERVINGS

PASTA SALAD

- 6 cups cooked regular or multigrain rotini pasta
- 1½ cups diced cucumber
- 1 cup diced tomatoes (about 2 medium)
- 1 cup diced green bell pepper (about 1 medium)
- 1 package (4 ounces) crumbled feta cheese
- 12 medium pitted black olives, sliced
- ¼ cup chopped fresh dill

DRESSING

- ¼ cup extra virgin olive oil
- ¼ cup fresh lemon juice
- ¼ teaspoon salt
- ¼ teaspoon dried oregano
- ⅛ teaspoon black pepper

1. For pasta salad, combine pasta, cucumber, tomatoes, bell pepper, feta cheese, olives and dill in large bowl.

2. For dressing, whisk oil, lemon juice, salt, oregano and black pepper in small bowl. Pour over salad; toss well. Refrigerate until ready to serve.

TOMATO AND BRIE PASTA

MAKES 6 SERVINGS

1 pint grape tomatoes, halved lengthwise

2 teaspoons olive oil

¾ teaspoon salt, divided

4 cups uncooked egg noodles

2 tablespoons butter

1 clove garlic, smashed

2 tablespoons all-purpose flour

2 cups half-and-half, heated

8 ounces good-quality ripe Brie, crust removed, cut into small chunks

2 tablespoons minced fresh chives

¼ cup finely chopped fresh basil

¼ teaspoon black pepper

¼ cup sliced almonds

1. Preheat oven to 425°F. Line baking sheet with heavy-duty foil. Spray 9-inch square baking dish with nonstick cooking spray.

2. Spread tomatoes on prepared baking sheet. Drizzle with oil and sprinkle with ¼ teaspoon salt. Roast 20 minutes or until tender and slightly shriveled. Remove and set aside. *Reduce oven temperature to 350°F.*

3. Cook pasta according to package directions for al dente. Drain and set aside.

4. Melt butter in large saucepan or deep skillet over medium heat. Add garlic; cook 1 minute. Stir in flour until smooth paste forms. Gradually whisk in half-and-half; cook and stir until thickened. Discard garlic. Gradually stir in cheese until melted.

5. Add chives, basil, remaining ½ teaspoon salt and pepper. Stir in noodles. Drain off any liquid from tomatoes; fold into noodle mixture. Spread in prepared baking dish.

6. Bake 17 to 20 minutes or until sauce starts to bubble. Sprinkle with almonds; bake 8 to 10 minutes or until nuts turn light golden brown.

CLAM AND SPINACH SPAGHETTI

MAKES 2 SERVINGS

4 ounces uncooked multigrain or regular spaghetti

2 teaspoons olive oil

1 cup diced onion

¼ cup sliced green onions

1 clove garlic, minced

1 can (6½ ounces) clams, undrained

2 tablespoons grated Parmesan cheese

2 cups baby spinach leaves

2 tablespoons chopped fresh parsley

Salt and black pepper

1. Prepare pasta according to package directions. Drain and keep warm.

2. Meanwhile, heat oil in large skillet over medium heat. Add onion; cook and stir about 2 minutes or until translucent. Add green onions and garlic; cook and stir 1 minute.

3. Stir in clams with juice. Reduce heat to medium-low; cook 1 to 2 minutes. Stir in spinach. Cover and cook about 2 minutes or until spinach wilts.

4. Serve clam mixture over pasta. Sprinkle with Parmesan and parsley; season with salt and pepper.

PENNE WITH RICOTTA, TOMATOES AND BASIL

MAKES 4 SERVINGS

16 ounces uncooked penne pasta

1 can (28 ounces) diced Italian plum tomatoes, drained

1 container (15 ounces) ricotta cheese

⅔ cup chopped fresh basil

¼ cup olive oil

1 tablespoon balsamic vinegar

1 clove garlic, minced

1 teaspoon salt

¼ teaspoon red pepper flakes or black pepper

Grated Parmesan cheese

1. Cook pasta according to package directions; drain.

2. Meanwhile, combine tomatoes, ricotta cheese, basil, oil, vinegar, garlic, salt and red pepper flakes in large bowl; mix well.

3. Add pasta to ricotta mixture; toss gently to coat. Sprinkle with Parmesan cheese. Serve immediately.

MEDITERRANEAN ORZO AND VEGETABLE PILAF

MAKES 4 SERVINGS

¾ cup uncooked orzo pasta

2 teaspoons olive oil

1 small onion, diced

2 cloves garlic, minced

1 small zucchini, diced

½ cup fat-free reduced-sodium chicken broth

1 can (about 14 ounces) artichoke hearts, drained and quartered

1 medium tomato, chopped

½ teaspoon dried oregano

½ teaspoon salt

¼ teaspoon black pepper

½ cup crumbled feta cheese

Sliced black olives (optional)

1. Cook orzo according to package directions. Drain and set aside.

2. Heat oil in large nonstick skillet over medium heat. Add onion; cook and stir 5 minutes or until translucent. Add garlic; cook and stir 1 minute. Reduce heat to low. Add zucchini and broth; simmer 5 minutes or until zucchini is crisp-tender.

3. Add cooked orzo, artichokes, tomato, oregano, salt and pepper; cook and stir 1 minute or until heated through. Top with cheese and olives, if desired.

PAPPARDELLE WITH SHRIMP AND MIXED MUSHROOMS

MAKES 2 TO 4 SERVINGS

6 ounces uncooked pappardelle pasta

1 tablespoon olive oil

2 packages (4 ounces each) sliced exotic mushrooms *or* 1 package (8 ounces) sliced mushrooms

⅓ cup chopped shallots

4 cloves garlic, minced

¾ cup chicken broth

8 ounces raw medium shrimp, peeled and deveined

½ cup half-and-half

1 tablespoon all-purpose flour

2 tablespoons chopped fresh thyme

½ teaspoon salt

⅛ teaspoon black pepper

¼ cup shredded Parmesan cheese

Toasted pine nuts

1. Cook pasta according to package directions; keep warm.

2. Meanwhile, heat oil in large skillet over medium heat. Add mushrooms, shallots and garlic; cook and stir 3 minutes. Add broth; simmer 5 minutes. Add shrimp; cook 3 to 4 minutes or until shrimp are pink and opaque.

3. Whisk half-and-half and flour in small bowl until smooth and well blended; stir into shrimp mixture. Simmer 3 minutes or until sauce thickens slightly, stirring once. Stir in thyme, salt and pepper.

4. Divide pasta among serving plates. Top evenly with shrimp mixture, cheese and pine nuts, if desired.

PUTTANESCA WITH ANGEL HAIR PASTA

MAKES 4 TO 6 SERVINGS

2 tablespoons olive oil

2 anchovy fillets, chopped

3 cloves garlic, minced

2 tablespoons tomato paste

1 can (28 ounces) diced Italian plum tomatoes

1 teaspoon dried oregano

1 teaspoon dried basil
   Salt and black pepper

1 can (14 ounces) tomato sauce

½ cup pitted Greek olives, sliced or coarsely chopped

2 tablespoons rinsed and drained capers

½ to 1½ teaspoons red pepper flakes

1 pound uncooked fresh or dried angel hair pasta

1. Heat 2 tablespoons oil in skillet over medium-low heat. Add anchovies; cook 2 to 3 minutes, stirring occasionally. Add garlic; cook and stir just until lightly browned. Add tomato paste; cook and stir 2 minutes.

2. Stir in tomatoes, oregano and basil; season with salt and pepper. Increase heat to medium; cook, stirring occasionally about 30 minutes or until tomatoes break down and mixture becomes saucy.

3. Reduce heat to medium-low. Add tomato sauce, olives capers and red pepper flakes; simmer 10 minutes.

4. Meanwhile, bring large saucepan of salted water to a boil. Cook pasta according to package directions for al dente. Drain; toss with sauce.

CLASSIC PESTO WITH LINGUINE

MAKES 4 SERVINGS

12 ounces uncooked linguine

1 tablespoon butter

¼ cup plus 1 tablespoon olive oil, divided

2 tablespoons pine nuts

1 cup tightly packed fresh basil leaves

2 cloves garlic

¼ teaspoon salt

¼ cup grated Parmesan cheese

1½ tablespoons grated Romano cheese

1. Bring large saucepan of salted water to a boil. Cook pasta according to package directions for al dente; drain and return to saucepan. Add butter; toss to coat. Cover and keep warm.

2. Meanwhile, heat 1 tablespoon oil in small skillet over medium-low heat. Add pine nuts; cook and stir 30 to 45 seconds until lightly browned, shaking pan constantly. Transfer pine nuts and oil to food processor.

3. Add basil, garlic and salt. With motor running, add remaining ¼ cup oil in thin steady stream; process until evenly blended and pine nuts are finely chopped.

4. Add Parmesan and Romano cheeses; pulse just until blended.

5. Add sauce to pasta; toss until well coated. Serve immediately.

FETTUCCINE WITH VEGETABLE MARINARA SAUCE

MAKES 4 TO 6 SERVINGS

2 tablespoons extra virgin olive oil

1 medium yellow onion, finely chopped

1 carrot, finely chopped

1 stalk celery, finely chopped

2 cloves garlic, finely chopped

1 can (28 ounces) whole Italian plum tomatoes, undrained

½ cup water

⅓ cup packed chopped fresh basil leaves

Salt and freshly ground black pepper

1 pound uncooked fresh or dried fettuccine

2 tablespoons butter, thinly sliced

Shredded Parmesan cheese

1. Heat oil in large saucepan over medium heat. Add onion, carrot, celery and garlic; cover and cook about 5 minutes or until onion is golden and tender, stirring occasionally.

2. Drain tomatoes, reserving juice. Coarsely crush tomatoes with fingers or wooden spoon. Add tomatoes, reserved juice and water to saucepan; bring to a boil over high heat. Reduce heat to medium-low. Simmer, uncovered, about 45 minutes or until slightly thickened and reduced, stirring frequently. Stir in basil during last 5 minutes of cooking. Season to taste with salt and pepper.

3. Bring large saucepan of salted water to a boil. Cook pasta according to package directions for al dente. Drain and return to saucepan. Add butter; toss gently until pasta is coated and butter melts. Serve sauce over pasta; top with cheese.

FRESH VEGETABLE LASAGNA

MAKES 8 SERVINGS

- 8 ounces uncooked lasagna noodles
- 1 package (10 ounces) frozen chopped spinach, thawed and squeezed dry
- 1 cup shredded carrots
- ½ cup sliced green onions
- ½ cup sliced red bell pepper (1-inch pieces)
- ¼ cup chopped fresh parsley
- 1 teaspoon salt, divided
- ½ teaspoon black pepper
- 2 cups ricotta cheese
- ½ cup buttermilk
- 2 eggs
- 1 cup sliced mushrooms
- 1 can (14 ounces) artichoke hearts, rinsed, drained and chopped
- 2 cups (8 ounces) shredded mozzarella cheese
- ¼ cup grated Parmesan cheese

1. Cook pasta according to package directions. Rinse under cold water; drain well. Set aside.

2. Preheat oven to 375°F. Combine spinach, carrots, green onions, bell pepper, parsley, ½ teaspoon salt and black pepper in large bowl; set aside.

3. Combine ricotta cheese, buttermilk, eggs and remaining ½ teaspoon salt in food processor or blender. Process until smooth.

4. Spray 13×9-inch baking pan with nonstick cooking spray. Arrange one third of lasagna noodles in bottom of pan. Spread with half of cheese mixture, half of vegetable mixture, half of mushrooms, half of artichokes and ¾ cup mozzarella cheese. Repeat layers, ending with noodles. Sprinkle with remaining ½ cup mozzarella and Parmesan cheeses.

5. Cover; bake 30 minutes. Remove cover; bake 20 minutes or until bubbly and heated through. Let stand 10 minutes before cutting into pieces.

GRAINS, BEANS AND LEGUMES

CHEESY POLENTA

MAKES 6 SERVINGS

PREP TIME: 10 MINUTES
COOK TIME: 2 TO 2½ HOURS

- **6** cups vegetable broth
- **1½** cups uncooked medium-grind instant polenta
- **½** cup grated Parmesan cheese, plus additional for serving
- **4** tablespoons (½ stick) butter, cubed

Fried sage leaves (optional)

SLOW COOKER DIRECTIONS

1. Coat inside of slow cooker with nonstick cooking spray. Bring broth to a boil in large saucepan over high heat. Pour into slow cooker; whisk in polenta.

2. Cover; cook on LOW 2 to 2½ hours or until polenta is tender and creamy. Stir in ½ cup cheese and butter. Serve with additional cheese. Garnish with sage.

TIP: To make polenta on the stove, bring broth to a boil in large saucepan over high heat. Gradually whisk in polenta in thin steady stream. Cook 2 to 3 minutes or until thickened, whisking frequently. Reduce heat to low; cook about 45 minutes, stirring occasionally and adding water ½ cup at a time if polenta seems dry. Stir in cheese and butter just before serving. Spread any leftover polenta in a baking dish and refrigerate until cold. Cut cold polenta into sticks or slices. You can then fry or grill the polenta until lightly browned.

FARRO, CHICKPEA AND SPINACH SALAD

MAKES 4 TO 6 SERVINGS

1 cup uncooked pearled farro, rinsed

3 cups baby spinach, stemmed

1 medium cucumber, peeled and chopped

1 can (15 ounces) chickpeas, rinsed and drained

¾ cup pitted kalamata olives

¼ cup extra virgin olive oil

3 tablespoons white or golden balsamic vinegar or 3 tablespoons cider vinegar mixed with ½ teaspoon sugar

½ to 1 teaspoon chopped fresh rosemary

1 clove garlic, minced

1 teaspoon salt

⅛ to ¼ teaspoon red pepper flakes (optional)

½ cup crumbled goat cheese or feta cheese

1. Cook farro according to package directions; drain in fine-mesh strainer under cold running water to cool quickly.

2. Meanwhile, combine spinach, cucumber, chickpeas and olives in large bowl. Whisk oil, vinegar, rosemary, garlic, salt and red pepper flakes, if desired, in small bowl.

3. Stir farro into salad. Add dressing; stir until well blended. Fold in cheese.

BULGUR PILAF WITH KALE AND CARAMELIZED ONIONS

MAKES 4 SERVINGS

1 tablespoon olive oil

1 small onion, thinly sliced

1 clove garlic, minced

2 cups chopped kale

2 cups vegetable broth

¾ cup uncooked medium grain bulgur

½ teaspoon salt

¼ teaspoon black pepper

1. Heat oil in large nonstick skillet over medium heat. Add onion; cook about 8 minutes, stirring frequently or until softened and lightly browned. Add garlic; cook and stir 1 minute. Add kale; cook and stir about 1 minute or until kale is wilted.

2. Stir in broth, bulgur, salt and pepper. Bring to a boil. Reduce heat; cover and simmer 12 minutes or until liquid is absorbed and bulgur is tender.

MAKES 4 SERVINGS

2½ cups chopped plum tomatoes

1 cup cooked white beans

¼ cup chopped fresh basil

½ teaspoon salt

½ teaspoon black pepper

2 tablespoons olive oil, divided

1 package (16 ounces) prepared polenta, cut into ¼-inch-thick slices

¼ cup grated Parmesan cheese

1. Combine tomatoes, beans, basil, salt and pepper in medium bowl. Let stand at room temperature 15 minutes.

2. Heat 1 tablespoon oil in large nonstick skillet over medium-high heat. Add half of polenta slices; cook 4 minutes or until golden brown on both sides, turning once. Transfer to plate. Repeat with remaining oil and polenta.

3. Top with tomato mixture. Sprinkle with cheese.

FARRO RISOTTO WITH MUSHROOMS AND SPINACH

MAKES 4 SERVINGS

2 tablespoons olive oil

1 onion, chopped

12 ounces cremini mushrooms, stems trimmed and quartered

¾ teaspoon salt

¼ teaspoon black pepper

2 cloves garlic, minced

1 cup uncooked pearled farro

1 sprig fresh thyme

4 cups vegetable broth

8 ounces baby spinach

½ cup grated Parmesan cheese

1. Heat oil in large skillet or Dutch oven over medium heat. Add onion, mushrooms, salt and pepper; cook 6 to 8 minutes or until mushrooms have released their liquid and are browned, stirring occasionally. Add garlic; cook 1 minute. Stir in farro and thyme; cook 1 minute.

2. Add broth; bring to a boil. Reduce heat; cover and simmer 25 to 30 minutes or until farro is tender and broth is absorbed, stirring occasionally. Remove thyme sprig. Stir in spinach and cheese just before serving.

BULGUR, TUNA, TOMATO AND AVOCADO SALAD

MAKES 2 TO 3 SERVINGS

1 cup water

½ cup uncooked bulgur

1 cup halved grape tomatoes

1 can (6 ounces) tuna packed in water, drained and flaked

¼ cup finely chopped red onion

1 stalk celery, trimmed and thinly sliced

½ cup finely chopped avocado

1 tablespoon minced fresh parsley

2 tablespoons extra virgin olive oil

1 tablespoon fresh lemon juice

1 teaspoon white vinegar

½ teaspoon salt

⅛ teaspoon black pepper

1. Bring water to a boil in small saucepan. Stir in bulgur. Reduce heat to low; cover and simmer 8 minutes or until bulgur swells and has absorbed most of the water. Remove from heat; let stand 10 minutes.

2. Combine tomatoes, tuna, onion and celery in large bowl. Stir in bulgur, avocado and parsley. Whisk oil, lemon juice, vinegar, salt and pepper in small bowl. Pour over salad. Toss gently to mix. Chill 2 hours before serving.

ROSEMARY, HARICOTS VERTS AND GOAT CHEESE QUINOA

MAKES 6 SERVINGS

1 cup uncooked tri-colored quinoa

2 cups vegetable broth

1 tablespoon chopped fresh rosemary

1 package (12 ounces) fresh haricots verts, cut in half

3 tablespoons extra virgin olive oil

1 tablespoon Dijon mustard

1 tablespoon fresh lemon juice

1 teaspoon honey

¼ teaspoon salt

⅛ teaspoon black pepper

½ cup toasted pecan pieces*

1 container (4 ounces) goat cheese crumbles

To toast pecans, spread in single layer in heavy skillet. Cook over medium heat 1 to 2 minutes or until nuts are lightly browned, stirring frequently. Remove from skillet. Cool completely.

1. Place quinoa in fine-mesh strainer; rinse well under cold running water.

2. Combine quinoa and broth in medium saucepan; bring to a boil over high heat. Reduce heat to low; cover and simmer 15 to 20 minutes or until quinoa is tender and broth is absorbed. Add rosemary and haricots verts during last 5 minutes of cooking. Remove from heat; cool slightly.

3. Whisk oil, mustard, lemon juice, honey, salt and pepper in small bowl.

4. Place quinoa mixture in large bowl. Add dressing and pecans; toss until blended. Sprinkle with goat cheese before serving.

GREEK WHITE BEAN RISOTTO

MAKES 4 TO 6 SERVINGS

5 cups vegetable broth

2 tablespoons olive oil

3 cloves garlic, minced

1½ cups uncooked arborio rice

2 teaspoons dried oregano

⅓ cup finely chopped sun-dried tomatoes (not packed in oil)

1 cup cooked cannellini beans

¾ cup (3 ounces) crumbled feta cheese

⅓ cup grated Parmesan cheese

1 teaspoon fresh lemon juice

Salt and black pepper

1. Bring broth to a simmer in medium saucepan over medium-low heat.

2. Heat oil in large saucepan over medium heat. Add garlic; cook and stir 1 minute. Add rice and oregano; cook and stir 2 minutes or until rice is translucent. Add tomatoes.

3. Add broth, ½ cup at a time, stirring constantly until broth is absorbed before adding next ½ cup. Continue adding broth and stirring until rice is tender and mixture is creamy, about 20 to 25 minutes. Remove from heat.

4. Stir in beans; cook 1 minute, stirring constantly. Remove from heat. Stir in cheeses and lemon juice. Season with salt and pepper. Cover; let stand 5 minutes. Stir before serving.

PESTO FARRO SALAD WITH SPRING VEGETABLES AND FETA

MAKES 4 SERVINGS

½ cup packed fresh Italian parsley

2 cups packed fresh basil leaves

¼ cup toasted walnuts

2 cloves garlic

½ cup extra virgin olive oil

½ cup grated Parmesan cheese
  Salt and black pepper

1 cup uncooked pearled farro

1 cup fresh or frozen peas

1 bunch asparagus, trimmed and
  cut into 1-inch pieces

½ cup crumbled feta cheese

1. For pesto, place parsley, basil, walnuts and garlic in food processor. Pulse until mixture is coarsely chopped. With motor running, drizzle in oil in thin steady stream. Add Parmesan cheese; pulse to combine. Season with salt and pepper. Set aside.

2. Bring large saucepan of water to a boil over high heat. Add farro; reduce heat to medium-low. Cook about 30 minutes or until tender, adding peas during last 5 minutes of cooking time and asparagus during last 2 minutes of cooking time. Drain and place in large bowl.

3. Add ¾ cup pesto; toss to coat. (Reserve remaining pesto for another use.) Add feta cheese; stir until combined. Season with additional salt and pepper.

KOSHARI

PREP TIME: 40 MINUTES
COOK TIME: 3 HOURS

- 4 **cups water**
- 1 **cup uncooked white basmati rice, rinsed and drained**
- 1 **cup brown lentils, rinsed and sorted**
- 3 **teaspoons kosher salt, divided**
- ½ **teaspoon ground cinnamon**
- ½ **teaspoon ground nutmeg, divided**
- 1 **cup uncooked elbow macaroni**
- ¼ **cup olive oil**
- 1 **large onion, thinly sliced**
- 1 **large onion, diced**
- 1 **tablespoon minced garlic**
- 1 **teaspoon ground cumin**
- ½ **teaspoon ground coriander**
- ¼ **teaspoon red pepper flakes**
- ¼ **teaspoon black pepper**
- 1 **can (28 ounces) crushed tomatoes**
- 2 **teaspoons red wine vinegar**

SLOW COOKER DIRECTIONS

1. Place water, rice, lentils, 2 teaspoons salt, cinnamon and ¼ teaspoon nutmeg in slow cooker. Cover; cook on HIGH 2 hours 30 minutes. Stir in macaroni. Cover; cook 30 minutes, stirring halfway through cooking time.

2. Meanwhile, heat oil in large skillet over medium-high heat. Add sliced onion; cook 12 minutes or until edges are dark brown and onion is softened. Transfer onions to medium bowl using tongs or slotted spoon. Season with ¼ teaspoon salt. Set aside.

3. Heat same skillet with oil over medium heat. Add diced onion; cook and stir 8 minutes or until softened. Add garlic, cumin, coriander, cinnamon, red pepper flakes, black pepper and remaining ¼ teaspoon nutmeg; cook 30 seconds or until fragrant. Stir in tomatoes, vinegar and remaining ¾ teaspoon salt; cook 8 to 10 minutes or until thickened, stirring occasionally.

4. Lightly fluff rice mixture with fork. Place in bowls; top with sauce and fried onions.

VEGGIE-QUINOA AND BROWN RICE PILAF

MAKES 4 TO 6 SERVINGS

2 cups water

1 cup instant brown rice

½ cup uncooked tri-color, red or white quinoa

½ cup pine nuts or slivered almonds

2 tablespoons olive oil, divided

1 cup chopped onions

1 package (8 ounces) sliced cremini mushrooms

1 clove garlic, minced

½ cup finely chopped red bell pepper or seeded diced tomato

1 teaspoon chopped fresh rosemary

¾ teaspoon salt

Black pepper

¼ cup crumbled blue cheese

1. Bring water to a boil in medium saucepan over high heat. Stir in rice and quinoa. Reduce heat to low; cover and simmer 12 minutes or until water is absorbed.

2. Meanwhile, heat large skillet over medium-high heat. Add pine nuts; cook 1½ to 2 minutes or until just beginning to brown, stirring constantly. Transfer to plate to cool.

3. Heat 1 tablespoon oil in same skillet over medium-high heat. Add onions; cook and stir 6 minutes or until beginning to brown. Stir in mushrooms; cook 5 to 6 minutes or until beginning to brown on edges. Stir in garlic; cook 15 seconds, stirring constantly. Remove from heat.

4. Stir in remaining 1 tablespoon oil, bell pepper, rosemary, salt, rice mixture and pine nuts. Season with black pepper. Sprinkle with cheese.

BREADS, PIZZA AND SANDWICHES

FLATBREAD WITH HERBED RICOTTA, PEACHES AND ARUGULA

MAKES 4 SERVINGS

½ **cup ricotta cheese**

½ **teaspoon coarse salt**

⅛ **teaspoon black pepper**

2 **tablespoons finely chopped fresh basil**

2 **whole wheat naan breads or 4 whole wheat pita breads**

1 **ripe peach, cut into 12 slices**

½ **cup arugula**

½ **teaspoon fresh lemon juice**

1 **teaspoon extra virgin olive oil**

2 **teaspoons balsamic vinegar**

Flaky sea salt, for sprinkling

1. Preheat oven to 400°F. Line baking sheet with parchment paper.

2. Combine ricotta cheese, coarse salt, pepper and basil in small bowl. Spread mixture evenly on each piece of naan. Arrange peaches on top. Bake 12 minutes or until bottom of naan is crisp.

3. Combine arugula, lemon juice and oil in medium bowl; toss gently. Top baked flatbreads with arugula. Drizzle with vinegar and sprinkle with salt flakes. Cut into pieces to serve.

MEDITERRANEAN VEGETABLE SANDWICH

MAKES 4 SANDWICHES

½ cup plain hummus

½ jalapeño pepper, seeded and minced

¼ cup minced fresh cilantro

8 slices whole wheat bread

4 leaves lettuce (leaf or Bibb lettuce)

2 tomatoes, thinly sliced

½ cucumber, thinly sliced

½ red onion, thinly sliced

½ cup thinly sliced peppadew peppers or sweet Italian peppers

4 tablespoons crumbled feta cheese

1. Combine hummus, jalapeño and cilantro in small bowl; mix well.

2. Spread about 1 tablespoon hummus mixture on one side of each bread slice. Layer half of bread slices with lettuce, tomatoes, cucumber, onion, peppadew peppers and feta cheese; top with remaining bread slices. Cut sandwiches in half.

TOMATO AND CHEESE FOCACCIA

MAKES 1 LOAF

1 package (¼ ounce) active dry yeast

¾ cup warm water (105° to 115°F)

2 cups all-purpose flour

½ teaspoon salt

4 tablespoons olive oil, divided

1 teaspoon dried Italian seasoning

8 oil-packed sun-dried tomatoes, well drained

½ cup (2 ounces) shredded provolone cheese

¼ cup grated Parmesan cheese

1. Dissolve yeast in warm water in small bowl; let stand 5 minutes. Combine flour and salt in food processor. Add yeast mixture and 3 tablespoons oil; process until ingredients form a ball. Process 1 minute.

2. Turn dough out onto lightly floured surface. Knead about 2 minutes or until smooth and elastic. Place dough in oiled bowl; turn to grease top. Cover and let rise in warm place about 30 minutes or until doubled in size.

3. Punch down dough. Let rest 5 minutes. Press dough into oiled 10-inch round cake pan, cast iron skillet or springform pan. Brush with remaining 1 tablespoon oil; sprinkle with Italian seasoning. Press sun-dried tomatoes into top of dough; sprinkle with cheeses. Cover and let rise in warm place 15 minutes.

4. Preheat oven to 425°F. Bake 20 to 25 minutes or until golden brown. Cut into wedges to serve.

TIP: If mixing dough by hand, combine flour and salt in large bowl. Stir in yeast mixture and 3 tablespoons oil until a ball forms. Turn out onto lightly floured surface and knead about 10 minutes or until smooth and elastic. Proceed as directed.

SOCCA
(NIÇOISE CHICKPEA PANCAKE)

MAKES 6 SERVINGS

1 cup chickpea flour

¾ teaspoon salt

½ teaspoon black pepper

1 cup water

5 tablespoons olive oil, divided

1½ teaspoons minced fresh basil *or*
½ teaspoon dried basil

1 teaspoon minced fresh rosemary
or ¼ teaspoon dried rosemary

¼ teaspoon dried thyme

1. Sift chickpea flour into medium bowl. Stir in salt and pepper. Gradually whisk in water until smooth. Stir in 2 tablespoons oil. Let stand at least 30 minutes.

2. Preheat oven to 450°F. Place 9- or 10-inch cast iron skillet in oven to heat.

3. Add basil, rosemary and thyme to batter; whisk until smooth. Carefully remove skillet from oven. Add 2 tablespoons oil to skillet, swirling to coat pan evenly. Immediately pour in batter.

4. Bake 12 to 15 minutes or until edge of pancake begins to pull away from side of pan and center is firm. Remove from oven. Preheat broiler.

5. Brush with remaining 1 tablespoon oil. Broil 2 to 4 minutes or until dark brown in spots. Cut into wedges. Serve warm.

TIP: To make a thinner, softer crêpe, just increase the amount of water in the recipe by about ¼ cup and cook in batches in a skillet.

FOCACCIA WITH ROSEMARY AND ROMANO

MAKES 8 TO 10 SERVINGS

PREP TIME: 1 HOUR 45 MINUTES
COOK TIME: 2 HOURS

1¼ cups warm water (100° to 110°F)

1 package (¼ ounce) active dry yeast

3 tablespoons extra virgin olive oil

1 tablespoon sugar

3 to 3½ cups all-purpose flour

1½ tablespoons finely chopped fresh rosemary

1½ teaspoons salt

½ teaspoon red pepper flakes

¼ cup grated Romano cheese

SLOW COOKER DIRECTIONS

1. Coat inside of slow cooker with nonstick cooking spray. Combine water, yeast, oil and sugar in small bowl; let stand 5 minutes until foamy.

2. Combine flour, rosemary, salt and red pepper flakes in large bowl; stir to blend. Add yeast mixture; stir until soft dough forms. Turn dough out onto lightly floured surface; knead 5 minutes. Place dough in slow cooker; stretch to fit bottom. Cover; let stand 1 to 1½ hours in warm place until doubled in size.

3. Gently press dough with fingertips to deflate. Sprinkle with cheese. Cover; let rise 30 minutes. Place clean dry towel over top of slow cooker, then replace the lid.

4. Cover; cook on HIGH 2 hours or until dough is lightly browned on sides. Remove to wire rack. Let stand 10 to 15 minutes before slicing.

MEDITERRANEAN FLATBREAD

MAKES 16 PIECES

**Basic Pizza Dough (page 165)
or 1 package (11 ounces)
refrigerated French bread
dough**

2 **tablespoons olive oil, divided**

½ **cup thinly sliced yellow onion**

½ **cup thinly sliced red bell pepper**

½ **cup thinly sliced green bell
pepper**

2 **cloves garlic, minced**

½ **teaspoon dried rosemary**

⅛ **teaspoon red pepper flakes
(optional)**

⅓ **cup coarsely chopped pitted
kalamata olives**

¼ **cup grated Parmesan cheese**

1. Prepare pizza dough through step 2. Lightly grease baking sheet or line with parchment paper.

2. Preheat oven to 350°F. Thinly roll out dough to desired thickness on lightly floured surface. Place on prepared baking sheet.

3. Heat 1 tablespoon oil in large skillet over medium-high heat. Add onion and bell peppers; cook and stir 5 minutes or until onion begins to brown. Remove from heat.

4. Combine garlic and remaining 1 tablespoon oil in small bowl; spread evenly over dough. Sprinkle with rosemary and red pepper flakes, if desired. Top with onion mixture; sprinkle with olives.

5. Bake 16 to 18 minutes or until golden brown. Sprinkle with cheese. Cool on wire rack. Cut flatbread in half lengthwise; cut crosswise into 1-inch-wide strips.

BASIC PIZZA DOUGH

3   cups all-purpose flour

1   package (¼ ounce) rapid-rise active dry yeast

1   teaspoon salt

1   cup warm water (120°F)

2   tablespoons olive oil

1. Combine flour, yeast and salt in large bowl of stand mixer. Stir in water and olive oil to form rough dough. Knead with dough hook at low speed 5 to 7 minutes or until dough is smooth and elastic.

2. Shape dough into a ball. Place in greased bowl; turn to grease top. Cover and let rise in warm place about 45 minutes or until doubled in size. Punch down dough.

3. Shape into a ball; wrap in plastic wrap and refrigerate until ready to use.

SALAD-TOPPED FOCACCIA ROUNDS

MAKES 4 SERVINGS

1 **package (11 ounces) refrigerated French bread dough***

½ **cup thinly sliced red onion, divided**

¼ **to ½ teaspoon dried rosemary**

4 **cups spring greens**

3 **tablespoons vinaigrette or Italian Salad Dressing (page 51)**

½ **cup crumbled feta cheese**

Or use Basic Pizza Dough (page 165) prepared through step 2.

1. Preheat oven to 350°F. Lightly spray baking sheet with nonstick cooking spray.

2. Roll out dough on lightly floured surface. Cut dough into 4 squares. Shape into 4 rough circles about 4 inches in diameter. Sprinkle with rosemary and press ¼ cup onion into dough. Place on prepared baking sheet. Bake 12 to 14 minutes or until bottoms are lightly browned. Cool on wire rack 5 minutes.

3. Combine spring greens, remaining ¼ cup onion and vinaigrette in medium bowl. Toss to coat. Place 1 cup salad on each piece of bread; top with cheese.

CHICKEN TZATZIKI PITAS

MAKES 4 SERVINGS

½ cup plain Greek yogurt

¼ cup finely chopped cucumber

2 teaspoons fresh lemon juice

2 teaspoons chopped fresh mint

1 clove garlic, crushed

¼ teaspoon salt

Dash black pepper

2 (6-inch) whole wheat pita breads

1 cup chopped cooked chicken

1 cup chopped romaine lettuce

½ cup chopped fresh tomatoes

2 tablespoons chopped red onion

2 tablespoons chopped Greek olives

1. Stir together yogurt, cucumber, lemon juice, mint, garlic, salt and pepper in small bowl.

2. Cut pita breads in half. Divide chicken, lettuce, tomatoes, onion and olives evenly among pita halves. Drizzle with sauce.

SUN-DRIED TOMATO, CHICKEN SAUSAGE, FENNEL AND APPLE FLATBREAD

MAKES 6 SERVINGS

2 tablespoons sun-dried tomato dressing

1 (10½-ounce) stone-baked pizza crust*

1 small red onion, thinly sliced

½ fennel bulb, thinly sliced

1 fully-cooked sun-dried tomato chicken sausage, thinly sliced

1 Granny Smith apple, peeled, cored and thinly sliced

¾ cup (3 ounces) finely shredded mozzarella cheese

2 tablespoons grated Parmesan cheese

*Or use Basic Pizza Dough (page 165) prepared through step 2. Thinly roll out dough to desired thickness on lightly floured surface. Place on greased baking sheet.

1. Heat oven to 400°F. Spread dressing over crust.

2. Layer onion, fennel, chicken sausage and apple over crust. Sprinkle evenly with cheeses.

3. Bake 20 minutes or until cheeses are melted and crust is golden brown.

GREEK SPINACH AND FETA PIE

MAKES 6 SERVINGS

⅓ cup butter, melted

2 eggs

1 container (15 ounces) ricotta cheese

1 package (10 ounces) frozen chopped spinach, thawed and squeezed dry

1 package (4 ounces) crumbled feta cheese

¾ teaspoon finely grated lemon peel

¼ teaspoon salt

¼ teaspoon black pepper

⅛ teaspoon ground nutmeg

1 package (16 ounces) frozen phyllo dough, thawed

1. Preheat oven to 350°F. Brush 13×9-inch baking dish lightly with some of butter.

2. Beat eggs in medium bowl. Stir in ricotta, spinach, feta, lemon peel, salt, pepper and nutmeg. Set aside.

3. Unwrap phyllo dough; remove 8 sheets. Cut dough in half crosswise forming 16 rectangles about 13×8½ inches. Cover dough with damp cloth or plastic wrap to keep moist while assembling pie. Reserve remaining dough for another use.

4. Place 1 piece of phyllo in prepared dish; brush top lightly with butter. Layer with another piece of phyllo and brush lightly with butter. Continue layering with 6 pieces of phyllo, brushing each lightly with butter. Spoon spinach mixture evenly over phyllo.

5. Top spinach mixture with piece of phyllo; brush lightly with butter. Repeat layering with remaining 7 pieces of phyllo, brushing each piece lightly with butter.

6. Bake 35 to 40 minutes or until golden brown.

FRUIT AND DESSERTS

POMEGRANATE AND ORANGE SHERBET

MAKES ABOUT 1½ QUARTS

⅔ **cup sugar**

2 **cups bottled pomegranate juice**

1 **cup fresh orange juice**

2 **teaspoons grated orange peel**

2 **tablespoons grenadine (optional)**

1. Bring sugar and ⅔ cup water to a boil in small saucepan over high heat, stirring to dissolve sugar. Boil 5 minutes or until syrup is slightly thickened. Cool slightly.

2. Combine pomegranate juice, orange juice, orange peel, and grenadine, if desired, in medium bowl. Stir in sugar syrup. Cool in refrigerator at least 2 hours.

3. Freeze mixture in ice cream maker according to manufacturer's directions until soft.

4. Transfer sherbet to freezer containers. Freeze at least 2 hours or until firm.

ORANGE CAKE

1½ cups all-purpose flour

1 cup sugar

   Grated peel of 1 orange

1 teaspoon baking soda

¼ teaspoon salt

1 cup orange juice

5 tablespoons vegetable or olive oil

   Orange Frosting (recipe follows, optional)

   Candied orange peel (optional)

1. Preheat oven to 350°F. Spray 9-inch round cake pan with nonstick cooking spray.

2. Combine flour, sugar, orange peel, baking soda and salt in medium bowl. Combine orange juice and oil in small bowl or measuring cup. Add to flour mixture; stir until smooth. Spread batter in prepared pan.

3. Bake 30 minutes or until toothpick inserted into center comes out clean. Cool cake in pan 10 minutes; remove to wire rack to cool completely.

4. Meanwhile, prepare frosting, if desired. Frost cake; garnish with candied orange peel.

ORANGE FROSTING

½ cup (1 stick) butter

2 teaspoons grated orange peel

2 tablespoons orange juice

1 teaspoon vanilla

4 cups powdered sugar

4 to 6 tablespoons milk or whipping cream

1. Beat butter in medium bowl with electric mixer at medium speed until light and fluffy. Beat in orange peel, orange juice and vanilla.

2. Gradually beat in powdered sugar. Beat in milk by tablespoonfuls until spreading consistency is reached.

GRAPEFRUIT SORBET

MAKES 4 SERVINGS

1 **large pink grapefruit**

½ **cup apple juice**

1½ **tablespoons sugar**

1. Peel grapefruit and remove white pith. Cut into segments over bowl to catch juices, removing membranes between segments. Combine grapefruit, grapefruit juice, apple juice and sugar in food processor or blender; purée until smooth.

2. Freeze grapefruit mixture in ice cream maker according to manufacturer's directions. Serve immediately.

PLUM-GINGER BRUSCHETTA

MAKES 9 SERVINGS

1 sheet frozen puff pastry (half of 17¼-ounce package)

2 cups chopped unpeeled firm ripe plums (about 3 medium)

2 tablespoons sugar

2 tablespoons chopped candied ginger

1 tablespoon all-purpose flour

2 teaspoons fresh lemon juice

⅛ teaspoon ground cinnamon

2 tablespoons apple jelly or apricot preserves

1. Unfold puff pastry and thaw 30 minutes on lightly floured work surface. Preheat oven to 400°F. Line baking sheet with parchment paper.

2. Cut puff pastry sheet lengthwise into 3 strips. Cut each strip crosswise in thirds to make 9 pieces. Place on prepared baking sheet. Bake 10 minutes or until puffed and lightly browned.

3. Meanwhile, combine plums, sugar, ginger, flour, lemon juice and cinnamon in medium bowl.

4. Gently brush each piece puff pastry with ½ teaspoon jelly; top with scant ¼ cup plum mixture. Bake about 12 minutes or until fruit is tender.

BAKLAVA

4 cups walnuts, shelled pistachios
   and/or slivered almonds
   (1 pound)

1¼ cups sugar, divided

2 teaspoons ground cinnamon

½ teaspoon salt

¼ teaspoon ground cloves

1 package (16 ounces) frozen
   phyllo dough, thawed

1 cup (2 sticks) butter, melted

1½ cups water

¾ cup honey

2 (2-inch-long) strips lemon peel

1 tablespoon fresh lemon juice

1 cinnamon stick

3 whole cloves

1. Place half of walnuts in food processor. Pulse until nuts are finely chopped, but not pasty. Transfer to large bowl; repeat with remaining nuts. Add ½ cup sugar, ground cinnamon, salt and ground cloves to nuts; mix well.

2. Preheat oven to 325°F. Brush 13×9-inch baking dish with some of melted butter or line with foil, leaving overhang on two sides for easy removal. Unroll phyllo dough and place on large sheet of waxed paper. Trim phyllo sheets to 13×9 inches. Cover phyllo with plastic wrap and damp clean kitchen towel. (Phyllo dough dries out quickly if not covered.)

3. Place 1 phyllo sheet in bottom of dish, folding in edges if too long; brush surface with butter. Repeat with 7 phyllo sheets, brushing surface of each sheet with butter. Sprinkle about ½ cup nut mixture evenly over layered phyllo. Top nuts with 3 more layers of phyllo, brushing each sheet with butter. Sprinkle another ½ cup nut mixture on top. Repeat layering and brushing of 3 phyllo sheets with ½ cup nut mixture until there are a total of eight 3-sheet layers. Top final layer of nut mixture with remaining 8 phyllo sheets, brushing each sheet with butter.

4. Score baklava lengthwise into 4 equal sections, then cut diagonally at 1½-inch intervals to form diamond shapes. Sprinkle top lightly with some water to prevent top phyllo layers from curling up during baking. Bake 50 to 60 minutes or until golden brown.

5. Meanwhile, combine 1½ cups water, remaining ¾ cup sugar, honey, lemon peel, lemon juice, cinnamon stick and whole cloves in medium saucepan. Bring to a boil over high heat. Reduce heat to low; simmer 15 minutes. Strain hot syrup; drizzle evenly over hot baklava. Cool completely. Cut into pieces along score lines.

PLUM AND WALNUT PIE

MAKES 8 SERVINGS

Single-Crust Pie Pastry (recipe follows)

STREUSEL TOPPING

- ¼ **cup all-purpose flour**
- ¼ **cup old-fashioned oats**
- ¼ **cup granulated sugar**
- ¼ **cup packed brown sugar**
- ⅛ **teaspoon salt**
- ¼ **cup (½ stick) cold butter, cubed**

PIE FILLING

- 8 **cups thinly sliced plums**
- ⅓ **cup granulated sugar**
- ⅓ **cup packed brown sugar**
- 3 **to 4 tablespoons all-purpose flour**
- 1 **tablespoon honey**
- ½ **teaspoon ground cinnamon**
- ¼ **teaspoon ground ginger**
- ⅛ **teaspoon salt**
- ½ **cup candied or plain walnuts**

1. Prepare pie pastry.

2. For streusel topping, combine ¼ cup all-purpose flour, ¼ cup old-fashioned oats, ¼ cup granulated sugar, ¼ cup packed light brown sugar and ⅛ teaspoon salt in medium bowl. Add butter; crumble with fingertips until mixture resembles coarse crumbs.

3. Preheat oven to 425°F. For filling, combine plums, ⅓ cup granulated sugar, ⅓ cup brown sugar, 3 tablespoons flour (use 4 tablespoons if plums are very juicy), honey, cinnamon, ginger and ⅛ teaspoon salt in large bowl; toss to coat.

4. Roll out pastry into 11-inch circle on floured surface. Line 9-inch pie pan with pastry; flute edge. Spread plum mixture evenly in crust; sprinkle with streusel. Place pie on baking sheet.

5. Bake 15 minutes. *Reduce oven temperature to 350°F.* Sprinkle pie with walnuts. Bake 30 minutes. Lightly tent pie with foil. Bake 30 minutes or until filling is bubbly and crust is golden brown. Let stand at least 30 minutes before slicing.

TIP: Candied walnuts are sold in packages in the baking section of the supermarket; they may also be found in the produce section where salad ingredients are sold.

SINGLE—CRUST PIE PASTRY
MAKES PASTRY FOR ONE 9-INCH PIE

1¼ **cups all-purpose flour**

½ **teaspoon salt**

3 **tablespoons shortening***

3 **tablespoons cold unsalted butter,
   cubed**

3 **to 4 tablespoons ice water**

½ **teaspoon cider vinegar**

*Or use 6 tablespoons cold butter instead of
shortening and butter.*

1. Combine flour and salt in medium bowl. Cut in shortening and butter with pastry blender or two knives until mixture resembles coarse crumbs. Combine 3 tablespoons water and vinegar in small bowl. Add to flour mixture; mix with fork until dough forms, adding additional water as needed.

2. Shape dough into a disc; wrap in plastic wrap. Refrigerate 30 minutes.

KIWI AND STRAWBERRIES WITH PINE NUTS

MAKES 4 SERVINGS

2 **kiwi fruits**

1½ **cups fresh strawberries**

1 **tablespoon fresh orange juice**

1 **tablespoon pine nuts, toasted**

1. Peel kiwis and slice into thin rounds. Arrange on 4 dessert plates.

2. Hull and slice strawberries. Arrange over kiwi slices. Drizzle orange juice evenly over fruit; top with pine nuts.

POLENTA APRICOT PUDDING CAKE

MAKES 8 SERVINGS

¼ **cup chopped dried apricots**

1½ **cups fresh orange juice**

1 **cup ricotta cheese**

3 **tablespoons honey**

¾ **cup sugar**

⅔ **cup cornmeal**

½ **cup all-purpose flour**

½ **teaspoon salt**

¼ **teaspoon ground nutmeg**

½ **cup slivered almonds**

1. Preheat oven to 325°F. Spray 9-inch nonstick springform pan with nonstick cooking spray.

2. Soak apricots in warm water in small bowl 15 minutes to soften. Drain and pat dry. Set aside.

3. Beat orange juice, ricotta cheese and honey in large bowl with electric mixer at medium speed 2 to 3 minutes or until smooth. Combine sugar, cornmeal, flour, salt and nutmeg in medium bowl. Add to orange juice mixture; mix well. Stir in apricots. Pour into prepared pan. Sprinkle with almonds.

4. Bake 40 to 50 minutes or until center is almost set and cake is golden brown. Serve warm.

BERRY-PEACHY COBBLER

MAKES 8 SERVINGS

4 **tablespoons plus 2 teaspoons sugar, divided**

¾ **cup plus 2 tablespoons all-purpose flour, divided**

1¼ **pounds peaches, peeled and sliced *or* 1 package (16 ounces) frozen unsweetened sliced peaches, thawed and drained**

2 **cups fresh raspberries *or* 1 package (12 ounces) frozen unsweetened raspberries**

1 **teaspoon grated lemon peel**

½ **teaspoon baking powder**

½ **teaspoon baking soda**

⅛ **teaspoon salt**

2 **tablespoons cold butter, cut into small pieces**

¼ **cup plus 1 tablespoon buttermilk**

¼ **cup plain Greek yogurt**

1. Preheat oven to 425°F. Spray eight ramekins or one 11×7-inch baking dish with nonstick cooking spray; place ramekins in jelly-roll pan.

2. Combine 2 tablespoons sugar and 2 tablespoons flour in large bowl. Add peaches, raspberries and lemon peel; toss to coat. Divide fruit evenly among prepared ramekins. Bake 15 minutes or until fruit is bubbly around edges.

3. Meanwhile, combine 2 tablespoons sugar, remaining ¾ cup flour, baking powder, baking soda and salt in medium bowl. Cut in butter with pastry blender or two knives until mixture resembles coarse crumbs. Stir in buttermilk and yogurt just until dry ingredients are moistened.

4. Remove ramekins from oven; drop batter onto fruit in dollops. Sprinkle with remaining 2 teaspoons sugar. Bake 18 to 20 minutes or until topping is lightly browned. Serve warm.

APRICOT TARTLETS

- **4 sheets frozen phyllo dough, thawed**
- **4 tablespoons melted butter**
- **1 can (15 ounces) apricot halves in juice, drained**
- **4 tablespoons apricot preserves**
- **1 tablespoon powdered sugar**
- **1 teaspoon ground cinnamon**

1. Preheat oven to 350°F. Line baking sheet with foil; spray foil with nonstick cooking spray.

2. Place one sheet of phyllo dough on work surface; keep remaining sheets covered with plastic wrap and damp clean towel. Brush phyllo dough with some of butter. Fold in half to create 8×6-inch rectangle; brush with butter.

3. Place 3 apricot halves, cut side up, in center of phyllo dough. Spread 1 tablespoon preserves over apricots. Fold and pleat about 1 inch of dough around edges to form round tartlet shell. Repeat with remaining ingredients to form 3 more tartlets. Place on prepared baking sheet.

4. Bake 22 minutes or until golden brown and crisp. Combine powdered sugar and cinnamon in small bowl; sprinkle over tartlets. Serve warm.

TIP: Phyllo dough dries out very quickly and crumbles easily. Keep thawed phyllo dough wrapped or covered until all the ingredients are assembled and you are ready to work with the dough.

METRIC CONVERSION CHART

VOLUME MEASUREMENTS (dry)

$^1/_8$ teaspoon = 0.5 mL
$^1/_4$ teaspoon = 1 mL
$^1/_2$ teaspoon = 2 mL
$^3/_4$ teaspoon = 4 mL
1 teaspoon = 5 mL
1 tablespoon = 15 mL
2 tablespoons = 30 mL
$^1/_4$ cup = 60 mL
$^1/_3$ cup = 75 mL
$^1/_2$ cup = 125 mL
$^2/_3$ cup = 150 mL
$^3/_4$ cup = 175 mL
1 cup = 250 mL
2 cups = 1 pint = 500 mL
3 cups = 750 mL
4 cups = 1 quart = 1 L

VOLUME MEASUREMENTS (fluid)

1 fluid ounce (2 tablespoons) = 30 mL
4 fluid ounces ($^1/_2$ cup) = 125 mL
8 fluid ounces (1 cup) = 250 mL
12 fluid ounces (1$^1/_2$ cups) = 375 mL
16 fluid ounces (2 cups) = 500 mL

WEIGHTS (mass)

$^1/_2$ ounce = 15 g
1 ounce = 30 g
3 ounces = 90 g
4 ounces = 120 g
8 ounces = 225 g
10 ounces = 285 g
12 ounces = 360 g
16 ounces = 1 pound = 450 g

DIMENSIONS

$^1/_{16}$ inch = 2 mm
$^1/_8$ inch = 3 mm
$^1/_4$ inch = 6 mm
$^1/_2$ inch = 1.5 cm
$^3/_4$ inch = 2 cm
1 inch = 2.5 cm

OVEN TEMPERATURES

250°F = 120°C
275°F = 140°C
300°F = 150°C
325°F = 160°C
350°F = 180°C
375°F = 190°C
400°F = 200°C
425°F = 220°C
450°F = 230°C

BAKING PAN SIZES

Utensil	Size in Inches/Quarts	Metric Volume	Size in Centimeters
Baking or Cake Pan (square or rectangular)	8×8×2	2 L	20×20×5
	9×9×2	2.5 L	23×23×5
	12×8×2	3 L	30×20×5
	13×9×2	3.5 L	33×23×5
Loaf Pan	8×4×3	1.5 L	20×10×7
	9×5×3	2 L	23×13×7
Round Layer Cake Pan	8×1½	1.2 L	20×4
	9×1½	1.5 L	23×4
Pie Plate	8×1¼	750 mL	20×3
	9×1¼	1 L	23×3
Baking Dish or Casserole	1 quart	1 L	—
	1½ quart	1.5 L	—
	2 quart	2 L	—